NOT JUST FOR SUPER CHRISTIANS

a 30-day adventure with *JESUS*

KEVIN SENAPATIRATNE

CHRIST CONNECTION
M·E·D·I·A

CHRIST CONNECTION
Blaine, MN 55434
www.christconnection.cc

Not Just for Super Christians: A 30-day adventure with Jesus

Copyright © 2018 Kevin Senapatiratne

ISBN 978-1-387-55438-6

Unless otherwise noted, Scripture quotations are from taken from the Holy Bible, NEW INTERNATIONAL VERSION®, NIV® Copyright © 1973, 1978, 1984, 2011 by Biblica, Inc.® Used by permission. All rights reserved worldwide.

Scripture quotations marked ESV are from The ESV® Bible (The Holy Bible, English Standard Version®), copyright © 2001 by Crossway, a publishing ministry of Good News Publishers. Used by permission. All rights reserved.

Cover photo: Sebastien Gabriel, Unsplash.com

Table of Contents

Introduction: I dare you ... 1
Day 1   How to Cross a Body of Water ... 4
Day 2   Lifestyle Design ... 8
Day 3   A Manifesto on Engagement ... 12
Day 4   The Power of Today ... 16
Day 5   The God Who Is Present ... 19
Day 6   Encourage Someone Today ... 23
Day 7   Humility – The Powerful Attitude to Accelerate Your Life ... 27
Day 8   You Are Not Going to Talk About Goals, Are You? ... 32
Day 9   Do Something Fun ... 36
Day 10 Simplicity and Organization ... 40
Day 11 Order Out of Chaos ... 45
Day 12 Enough ... 49
Day 13 Advisors ... 54
Day 14 Invest in Others ... 58
Day 15 Get a Passport ... 61
Day 16 Speak Wisely ... 65
Day 17 Shut It Off ... 68
Day 18 Give Something Away ... 71
Day 19 Pray for Someone ... 74

Day 20	Find Your True Source	*78*
Day 21	Do Something Extra for the Ministry You Serve	*81*
Day 22	Embrace Radical Obedience	*84*
Day 23	Deal with a Sin	*88*
Day 24	Take a Risk	*91*
Day 25	Face your Fears	*95*
Day 26	Make a Goodness and Mercy Timeline	*99*
Day 27	Enjoy Your Church	*103*
Day 28	Keep the Dream Alive	*106*
Day 29	Live with the Bible over a Lifetime	*110*
Day 30	Ask God for a Challenge	*114*

Curtain Call *117*

Introduction

I DARE YOU

People always ask me about the background of my last name. The story goes that my great-great grandfather in Sri Lanka thought his name was boring. He took two Sinhala words (Sinhala is one of the languages of Sri Lanka) and put them together to make a new name. Mission accomplished, great-great Grandpa—we no longer have a boring name!

With my unique last name and my family history, I have come to believe life should not be boring. And God did not design following Jesus to be boring. I love the quote attributed to Hunter Thompson: "Life should not be a journey to the grave with the intention of arriving safely in a pretty and well-preserved body, but rather to skid in broadside in a cloud of smoke, thoroughly used up, totally worn out, and loudly proclaiming 'Wow! What a ride!'"

As I travel to and speak at churches of all shapes and sizes, I find many Christians who are trying to follow Jesus, but if they were honest, have found their Christianity to be a little boring. Let me tell you: our faith was not designed to be that way.

I am here to get you back on the rollercoaster of a ride that is following Jesus. I want to challenge and help you get on the big slopes of life with Jesus.

Each day for the next 30 days, we are going to look at a story or principle from the Bible. Then, we are going to challenge you to put faith into action with a challenge. Some of you may remember the "choose-your-own-adventure" books that let you choose the story you wanted to read; imagine this book like that, but for your real life.

This is not a book designed to read a thought every day and think, "Hmm, that was nice" and put it down for the day. This is not like watching a movie where *someone else* works through their bucket list or says "yes" to new experiences. *You* are the main character in this drama (comedy?) of life you are living. This book is designed to get you back on stage.

> **GOD HAS PUT WITHIN OUR HEARTS THE DESIRE TO ENGAGE AND LIVE AN ADVENTURE.**

God has put within our hearts the desire to engage and live an adventure.

Before we get started, here are a few items to make this book more enjoyable and productive.

Find a partner to go through this book with you. Whenever I am challenging myself to do something, it is always more fun with a friend. It keeps me on track and also makes me feel better when I am doing something difficult to know that my friend has to do it as well! So, your first challenge for this book actually comes in the introduction. Contact a friend or group of friends and do this together. **Double-dog dare** them *if you have to.* You will be glad you did.

Keep what you've learned in your mind throughout the day. Meditate on the truths the Holy Spirit wants to teach you. Psalm 1 says whoever meditates on God's Word will prosper. Set a goal to think about the lesson or character as many times as possible during each 24-hour period. Make it a game for yourself to see how many times you can think about it.

Use the listening space. Each day has a space for you to write down the thoughts you have from God. Feel free to use this space as you like. Maybe, you will use it to write down your choice of challenge for the day. Maybe, the story from the Bible will spark a thought or an impression for your own life. Write it in the space. Use it to capture your journey or for a shopping list. Or, feel free to doodle in this space.

Don't forget to invite a friend on your adventure, and I will see you tomorrow.

Day 1

HOW TO CROSS A BODY OF WATER

Adventure. A word that can terrify and thrill us at the same time. Adventure takes us outside routine and comfort. And God seems to like that at times.

Take, for example, the simple idea of how to get across a body of water. We see this happen when the Israelites needed to get across the Red Sea with Pharaoh's armies closing in at the speed of chariot horses (Exodus 14). Hollywood has made some dramatic interpretations of this scene, but I am not sure even these truly capture the drama of the moment. With all eyes on Moses, he stretches his hand over the sea, and millions of gallons of water move by the hand of God.

I love even more what God does the next time they are trying to cross a body of water, this time the Jordan River (Joshua 3). Joshua could do what Moses did, but God commands him to do something different. This time, God asks him to lead the people to cross the body of water by first having the priests carry the ark into the water.

But God doesn't stop there. Later in the history of God's people, we see Israel's prophets, Elijah and Elisha, needing to again cross, you guessed it, a body of water. Elijah does neither of the things that have been done before. This time, he hits the water with his cloak (2 Kings 2:8). I picture him taking his cloak and hitting the water like when someone gets hit with a towel in the shower room. Ready for one last attempt to get across a body of water? Jesus walks *on* the water.

Each biblical water crossing profiled here was different, and this teaches us something. God sometimes does things the same way each time, and sometimes He wants us to experience what heart-pounding obedience looks like in a unique situation. Bible heroes couldn't simply take out their book, *7 Simple Steps to Crossing a Body of Water*. They had to walk in obedience to a creative and inspiring God.

> **THE KEY IN EXPERIENCING GOD'S GREAT POWER IS OBEDIENCE, LISTENING TO WHAT GOD COMMANDS.**

Remember, the key in experiencing God's great power is obedience, listening to what God commands. God may not have you cross a body of water today, but you might be surprised where He wants to take you when you are obedient. Commit now, no matter what He might say to you in the next 30 days, you will do it. If you don't feel comfortable that you hear God, stick with it, and you will grow in this area. (Interacting with the Bible is a great way to learn to hear God's voice).

Commit to the journey of adventure, wherever God would take you. You and the friend you are doing this book with may have different outcomes. Even if your entire church is going through this book, God is going to put his creative spin for each of your lives.

THOUGHT FOR THE DAY

God designed you to live in heart-pounding obedience as you follow Jesus.

Remember the choose-your-own-adventure part of this book? Most days, I'll give you three challenges to choose from for the day. Today, I give you one challenge with three options. Here it is.

A while back, I read an article by H.B. London on dangerous two-word prayers. In this adventurous spirit, pick one of the following prayers as a theme for your prayer today. Which challenge will you dare to pray today?

CHALLENGE 1

Pray, "God, stretch me!"

CHALLENGE 2

Pray, "God, lead me!"

CHALLENGE 3

Pray, "God, use me!"

BIBLE READING FOR TODAY

Isaiah 6

Jot down any impressions you feel God puts on your heart.

Day 2

LIFESTYLE DESIGN

Moses, Joshua, and Elijah are more than characters from your favorite show. Unlike popular fictional heroes, they did not arrive from the planet Krypton or sneak back from the land of Narnia. Instead, the people of the Bible were real people with real challenges, just like you. They had husbands, wives, daughters, sons, parents (and in-laws!) to deal with in their journey. If we could somehow give all of the people of the Bible a personality test, we would find a wide range of personalities, just like we encounter every day.

As you encounter people from the Bible in this book, or reading the Bible in general, attempt to engage with them as real people. Approach this book with curiosity, imagination, and an unhurried attitude you may not practice in your daily life. Ask yourself what it would be like to meet Bible characters in the grocery store or while out for a walk. What kind of conversation would you have with them?

Imagine for a moment sitting down with Noah from the Bible, and you're at your favorite lunch spot. What would you learn as you dive into a conversation? As Noah built his boat, I can only imagine that family reunions with the extended clan made for an interesting conversation. "Why are you building that thing, Noah?"

"All of the neighbors are giving us grief about your preaching style."

"That thing you are building is the strangest thing I have ever seen, Uncle Noah!"

As you and Noah order dessert, he challenges you to think about the importance of following your God-given path. If he had followed other people's desires for his life, where would we all be now? Just because other people hadn't built a boat didn't mean that he was not supposed to do *exactly that*. No one else was doing what he was doing.

> **IT MAY FEEL LIKE YOU ARE COLORING OUTSIDE THE LINES WHEN IT COMES TO THE LIFE GOD CALLS YOU TO LIVE.**

Sometimes, he says, you have to follow God in obedience for a long time without a lot of help from others.

Noah reminds you that you are responsible to live your life for God in the specific way He calls you to live. Prayer helps us come to Jesus to define what is most important for our individual story. Prayer connects us with the God who invites us to a journey of adventure with Him.

When Jesus called His disciples, He said, "Follow me" (Matthew 4:19). I love how Henry Blackaby and Claude King say it in *Experiencing God: Knowing and Doing the Will of God*: "He didn't give them a map, He said 'I am the way.'" That means, like I said yesterday, we are called to heart-pounding obedience to Him. You may be surprised by what kind of life he calls you to after you sit down to your planning meeting together. Noah was probably very surprised after God told him to build a boat. It may feel like you are coloring outside the lines when it comes to the life God calls you to live.

Remember, our primary goal in life is to build our relationship with Jesus. Paul said that, more than anything else in His life, he wanted to "know Christ" (Philippians 3:10). This is more than an intellectual exercise, but a desire for relationship. And this relationship is eternal. People often ask what you want people to say about you at the end of your life. But Christians design their lives with an answer to a more important, drastically life-changing question: "What do I want my life to say the first time I meet Jesus in eternity?"

THOUGHT FOR THE DAY

A walk with Jesus doesn't lead to an adventure, it is the adventure.

CHALLENGE 1

Set a timer for five minutes and write down a list of five things that you thought God might want you to do with your life, but you thought were impossible or crazy. Send the list to your friend who is doing the book with you and discuss it together.

CHALLENGE 2

Call the friend you are doing this book with and discuss stories of adventure when people follow God. Come up with stories you have heard in the Bible, in church history or people you have known personally. See how many you can come up with as you talk.

CHALLENGE 3

Noah's journey was very public to those around him. Publicly let people know that you are on a 30-day adventure with Jesus (maybe share through social media) and that you are excited to see where He takes you.

BIBLE READING FOR THE DAY

Philippians 3

Jot down any impressions you feel God puts on your heart.

Day 3

A MANIFESTO ON ENGAGEMENT

Yesterday, we imagined grabbing lunch and talking with Noah. In that same spirit, imagine you're hosting a brand-new podcast, with a twist: You have a time machine. You've seen time machines in TV, books, and movies. Now, you have your very own, meaning you can book any guest in the history of the world, and this time machine translates for you so you can talk to people from the past in their own language. Just schedule a time throughout history and meet people like Abraham Lincoln, Joan of Arc, or Julius Caesar. The people from the Bible would probably make especially exciting episodes.

You can interview all of the famous people of the Bible, but also the lesser-known players. The people who are not as well-known are fun because you get to dig a little deeper and stretch your research skills. Starting with a lesser known character, you pick the warrior, Caleb.

As Caleb walks into the room, you sense a different interview than you expected. Caleb puts down his weapons after he assesses the safety of the situation. Though his wrinkles show his age, his 85-year-old, muscular frame shows he has kept his body in peak condition over the years. And then in his eyes—there's a fire, and an intensity that is hard to deny. This is not a man who sat back and let life happen to him.

As Caleb begins to describe an experience he recently had, he comes alive. He is standing in front of his friend, Joshua. They have been friends for over 40 years. They have fought many battles together. The two of them stood up to a nation together when they explored the Promised Land (Numbers 13–14). Caleb describes to you how he asked Joshua for his inheritance, a land called Hebron (Joshua 14:13). You realize this is not the normal request of a man of 85—most men of Caleb's age are *giving* inheritances, not receiving them. Caleb reminded Joshua of the promise of God and wouldn't let anything keep him from that promise.

I see a recurring theme as I travel to churches of all shapes and sizes around the United States. The church seems to be missing the deep, passionate commitment of people like Caleb, a characteristic of following Jesus. Many church people, not "bad people," are going through the motions. Their journey has become routine. Dare I say their faith has become boring? They come to church on Sunday, they give in the offering, and they may even read their Bible every day. But something is missing. It's as if the Church is dating Jesus but has refused his proposal into the deeper life of marriage.

> **CALEB REMINDED JOSHUA OF THE PROMISE OF GOD AND WOULDN'T LET ANYTHING KEEP HIM FROM THAT PROMISE.**

One possible solution to these challenges is increased prayer resulting in increased mission. I have found as I challenge people to pray that prayer results in mission (By *mission*, I mean both the broader sense of God's activity for us and, more narrowly, the cross-cultural calling to bring the Gospel to new people).

Throughout history, when people come into the presence of God through prayer, God draws them into the mission He has for them. Then, as people engage in the mission God has for them, it becomes obvious to them they cannot complete it without the power of God realized through prayer.

So, mission drives you into the presence of God in prayer, and prayer drives you into mission. I have found they are interconnected and create momentum. It begins with you moving down the road of adventure and, very importantly, takes you to the heart of God. Caleb found this to be true.

So how do you become engaged? Like a groom love struck by his bride, you go *all in*. Caleb's challenge to us is to live our lives fully engaged.

THOUGHT FOR THE DAY

Half-hearted commitment to follow Jesus
keeps us "safe" but also keeps us from the adventure
we were designed to live.

CHALLENGE 1

If you have never been water baptized, contact your pastor to see when you can get baptized.

CHALLENGE 2

If you have been following Jesus for a while and just need to recommit to engaging like never before, be creative today. What fun way can you express your love for Jesus and following wherever He will take you?

CHALLENGE 3

If you had an idea from yesterday about your life that won't go away, take one small step to move in that direction today.

BIBLE READING FOR TODAY

Luke 9:57–62

Jot down any impressions you feel God puts on your heart.

Day 4

THE POWER OF TODAY

Yesterday, I introduced you to your time-traveling podcast where you interview people from the past using a time machine. The possibilities and conversations you could have would be truly life changing.

Imagine today you interview Moses. He's an old man but still as sharp as the man who stood up to the ruler of the world, the Egyptian Pharaoh, many years earlier in his life. You dive into your questions about the Plagues, Mount Sinai, and the crossing of the Red Sea, and you are not surprised by his answers. As you dig a little deeper, you are surprised when Moses begins to talk about his musical side.

You don't think about Moses as musical, but you remember hearing Psalm 90 attributed to him. One of the themes of that song is the shortness of life. He uses phrases like how people are "like the new grass." He mentions that our days "quickly pass." One of the most important lines seems to be, "Teach us to number our days aright, that we may gain a heart of wisdom."

You sense during the interview that Moses, who is close to 120, doesn't think all of those years seemed like a really long time. Life is short no matter how long you live. As you listen to Moses tell you about his unusual life, you notice again a commonality between the people you have met so far: *they all lived the life God gave them to live.*

How quickly life passes is a recurring theme in the Bible, but not many of us like to think about our own mortality. I once heard Pastor Andy Stanley say in a message about Psalm 90 that one trap we fall into when we don't value time is that we live to other people's expectations. But Moses tells us that when we number our days, we gain a heart of wisdom. That seems like something worth looking into more deeply.

> **HOW QUICKLY LIFE PASSES IS A RECURRING THEME IN THE BIBLE. BUT NOT MANY OF US LIKE TO THINK ABOUT OUR OWN MORTALITY.**

One of the great opportunities to engage and follow Jesus like we have talked about in previous days is to recapture the power of today. It does not mean that we don't plan or schedule anything beyond today, but we value the moments we have today and try to not miss out on what today holds.

Put another way, chefs say if you know how to make an egg, those fundamentals can advance into all manners of cooking. In our case, the "egg" is the value of a day. In later chapters, we will meet people who can help us understand the value of structuring our whole lives, but first we need to appreciate *one day*.

THOUGHT FOR THE DAY

Live out today as if it is the only day that you have, and you will become more grateful when you get another one.

CHALLENGE 1

Pray and write down what today could look like. What simple things could you add to today to make it special?

CHALLENGE 2

Who will you contact today that would make today interesting? What will you do to make it a little more unique?

CHALLENGE 3

What do you already have on your schedule today that, if you added a little extra effort, would bring joy or bring people closer to Jesus?

BIBLE READING FOR TODAY

Psalm 90

Jot down any impressions you feel God puts on your heart.

_____

_____

_____

_____

_____

_____

_____

Day 5

THE GOD WHO IS PRESENT

I love the little-talked-about people of the Bible. They may not have a lot of "TV time," so to speak, but they still have something to say. And even a brief cameo in the Bible plays out on the biggest stage of all time.

Enoch is a lesser-known character. From his prophecy quoted in Jude 1:14-15, we know there is more to his story than we read in the few verses in Genesis, but even those few verses challenge me. Genesis says that Enoch *walked with God*. What a compliment to be God's walking partner. The joy of journeying through life with God is a great statement. I would love that to be said about me. I would love to always be with God.

You might be asking, "Aren't we always with God?" You would be technically correct. Theologians use a fancy word to talk about God by speaking of his "omnipresence." It means that he is everywhere, all of the time. Yet, sometimes there is a truth of reality and then a truth of our experience. It makes me think of three stories in the Bible. Since you have a time machine to interview people for your podcast, you can talk to everyone involved.

The first person you interview is Jacob. You find him at an interesting time. He is *running for his dear life*. He has ticked off his brother, and his mother wisely sends him packing to a relative's house till Esau can calm down. Jacob doesn't know it will take Esau years to calm down, but he is running anyway. On his journey he stops for the night and uses a stone for a pillow. While sleeping he has an encounter with God. He wakes up and says, "Surely the Lord is in the place, and I was unaware of it" (Genesis 28:16). It wasn't that God wasn't there before, but Jacob was unaware of His presence.

> THE JOY OF JOURNEYING THROUGH LIFE WITH GOD IS A GREAT STATEMENT. I WOULD LOVE THAT TO BE SAID ABOUT ME. I WOULD LOVE TO ALWAYS BE WITH GOD.

The second person you interview is Elisha. Now, I am not sure if Elisha was reading and applying an adventure book like this one, but he is definitely *living* an adventure. He tells you how the king of Aram has been at war with Israel. Whenever the king makes a plan, Elisha has supernatural insight from God and tells it to the king of Israel. This goes on for a while until the king of Aram learns what is going on and gets mad. He sends an army to go and get Elisha.

The next morning Elisha's servant looks and sees an entire army assembled to get them—understandably, he freaks out a little bit. How would you feel if you woke up to an army out to get you? You might want a little more coffee! But Elisha prays, "Open his eyes, LORD, so that he may see" (2 Kings 6:17). Immediately, the servant is able to see the armies of heaven all around him, protecting them. Again, the army was already there, but he was unaware of them.

Your final interview is with Jesus' disciples, who have just learned some good news. They tell you how Jesus has just been killed, and they don't know what to make of it. Two disciples are going on a seven-mile journey out of Jerusalem. As they are

The God Who Is Present

walking along, Jesus walks up, but they don't recognize Him. After talking for a while, they stop for a meal. As Jesus blesses the food, they recognize Jesus just as he disappears. Their response is, "Were not our hearts burning within us . . .?" (Luke 24:32). Jesus was there, but they were not aware of Him.

Before we are too tough on Jesus' disciples, remember we can miss God all around us as well. It sometimes takes intention to avoid missing God. Frank Laubach, a missionary to the Philippines, tells of playing the "Game with Minutes" in the book *Letters from a Modern Mystic*. The idea was to try and see if he could, on any given day, draw his attention to God for one second of every minute of the day.

THOUGHT FOR THE DAY

*Awareness of the presence of God in our lives
can transform an ordinary day into an amazing day.*

After this lightning round of interviews for the podcast, let's play our own "Game with Minutes" and try to be more aware of God's presence in our own lives.

CHALLENGE 1

Set a timer of some sort to go off every hour for the rest of your day. When the timer goes off, take a moment to make yourself aware that God is with you.

CHALLENGE 2

Go somewhere in nature that makes you aware of the God who is everywhere. It doesn't have to be a trip to the Grand Canyon, but you could take a trip to the park or enjoy a YouTube video of nature.

CHALLENGE 3

Find some time to listen to some music that helps you become aware that God is near you.

BIBLE READING FOR TODAY

Revelation 4, a picture of the presence of God.

Jot down any impressions you feel God puts on your heart.

_____
_____
_____
_____
_____
_____
_____
_____
_____
_____

Day 6

ENCOURAGE SOMEONE TODAY

Sometimes, when the time machine is about to go to work, you wonder what takeaway the person you interview will bring to your podcast audience. Sometimes, the message of a person's life is obvious, and other times the application is less obvious.

When Ruth enters the room, you assume you already know the message of her life. The night before you had read the entire book of the Bible named after her. Ruth fell in love and married a man, then, he tragically died. But rather than going back to her old life, Ruth begins to follow her mother-in-law back to Israel and away from her Moabite homeland.

As you sit across from Ruth, you see the courage that drew her to change her whole life by following Naomi. She speaks simply about the choice to follow Naomi and her God. As you listen to her story, in many ways, the story is too ordinary for the makings of a Hollywood blockbuster. It is the simple story of man meets girl, man falls for girl, and then man finds a way to get the girl. There are no sword fights, explosions, or alien invasions.

Although her message is a love story, you want to dig deeper, to other lessons Ruth can teach your audience. One principle comes into view: *Boaz saw her need.* In your familiarity with the story, you had forgotten the desperate state in which Ruth and Naomi found themselves, practically speaking. In that culture women often depended on their husbands, or if not married, a male relative, for the resources they needed. Sitting across from Ruth, you sense how grateful she is for Boaz's care. He came to her help in her moment of need.

Ruth teaches us a simple act of kindness and encouragement can change a life.

Ruth changed Naomi's life by staying with her and not going back to her homeland. Ruth's love expressed for Naomi (shown in her not leaving her mother-in-law) made a difference.

Boaz changed Ruth and Naomi's life, and don't forget it brought him a wife. Boaz's practical care for Ruth became a love that changed both of their lives.

One of the challenges in expressing kindness is the need can seem overwhelming. Anyone can practice simple kindness, with an amazing impact. When we think about all the people we know, we may think, "There are so many people and so many opportunities." This can overwhelm us, and we end up doing nothing.

But here's how you counter that overwhelming feeling.

Realize that your job is not to do everything but to do something. Jesus said even a cup of cold water given in His name would not lose its reward (Mark 9:41). So even if you can't solve all the world's problems, you can

> **ANYONE CAN PRACTICE SIMPLE KINDNESS. WITH AN AMAZING IMPACT.**

make a differ-ence in one person's life today. That is a better place to start.

Allow prayer to enter your journey of encouragement. One of my favorite prayers in the Bible is Paul's prayer for the

Philippians: "And this is my prayer: that your love may abound more and more in knowledge and depth of insight, so that you may be able to discern what is best and may be pure and blameless for the day of Christ, filled with the fruit of righteousness that comes through Jesus Christ—to the glory and praise of God" (Philippians 1:9–11). This prayer is great because Paul is praying the love of the church in Philippi would get *smarter*, that when they are showing their love it would *make sense* and that they would be able to discern what is best. When we are faced with lots of opportunities to express love, Paul is showing by example that a good thing to do is pray that God helps you to express love best.

Before we finish today's illustration, it's worth talking about a great way to encourage others. Author David Jeremiah, in *The Power of Encouragement*, says that encouragement is speaking truth to people's fears. I think that is a great definition for how we can use our words to encourage others. When you think of someone in need, ask God what their fears are at this moment. When you realize the fear that they are experiencing at the moment, ask God to show you the truth of their situation. Maybe, a Scripture verse or a story from the Bible will come to mind. Then, think of the most loving and creative way to express that truth.

THOUGHT FOR THE DAY

Encouragement is the oxygen of the soul.
~ *John Maxwell*

CHALLENGE 1

Send a message of encouragement to someone who is struggling.

CHALLENGE 2

Send a message of encouragement to someone who is doing a great job.

CHALLENGE 3

Find a unique way to encourage someone today.

BIBLE READING FOR TODAY

Proverbs 25:25

Jot down any impressions you feel God puts on your heart.

_____
_____
_____
_____
_____
_____
_____
_____
_____

Day 7

HUMILITY: THE POWERFUL ATTITUDE TO ACCELERATE YOUR LIFE

Before we begin today, I need to remind you of something: I am a nerd. I enjoy things others might find strange. My hobbies include accelerated learning, mind mapping, memorization, and time management. In fact, I am so uncool I actually send myself an email every week reminding myself of my hobbies (because I haven't yet mastered my memorization hobby!).

For me, accelerated learning is any tool, system, or trick that helps you learn more quickly. One of the reasons for my interest in accelerated learning has to do with my first ministry position after college. Most people who leave a Bible college either start out as an associate pastor or pursue further studies. I jumped right into a senior pastor role in a local church. I actually started this position before I even graduated.

I was in over my head. Some days I was just trying to stay afloat. I even wore suits to give the (slight) impression I had it together. The church was in a small town five hours north of where I went to college. During travel time, I would listen to cassette tapes (now ancient technology!) to help me grow and be better. I listened through a lot of the nonfiction books they had at the library. Again, I realized that I needed help. The result of my accelerated learning experiment? It challenged me to grow and learn.

Now that I am on a challenge to engage 100,000 people to pray for their leaders, I am still in a little over my head. And although I've traded my cassette tapes for podcasts, I still feel a great need to learn. It reminds me of a little-talked about Bible story. For today's podcast, let's sit down with none other than Nebuchadnezzar, King of Babylon (now present-day Iraq) in the time after God's people were exiled to a foreign land.

With a last name like *Senapatiratne*, I am interested in people with long names. Among other things, King Nebuchadnezzar is infamous for throwing Daniel's friends into the fiery furnace. We won't go into that here because the next chapter of the story, detailed in Daniel 4, is just as interesting.

Nebuchadnezzar arrives from the time machine without the pomp you might expect from the leader of the known world at the time. Instead, he seems full of holy fear. He tells you about his dream in which God showed him that if he remained proud, he was going to end up eating grass like an animal for a while. "I did the bad thing," he says.

The king remained proud, and the mightiest man on earth assumed the role of a pasture-dwelling herbivore. After a time, Nebuchadnezzar gets the point. He acknowledged that God is in charge and gets his throne back. Because of God's humbling, Nebuchadnezzar seems less like a pagan, idol-worshipping king and more like someone who has just come through a great trial and lived to tell about it. One of the morals of this story, besides that

> **WHEN WE ACKNOWLEDGE OUR NEED FOR GOD, HE COMES NEAR TO US.**

humans are meant to eat things besides grass, is that pride is bad, and humility is good.

As Nebuchadnezzar leaves the interview to wash the grass stains out of his beard, let me nerd out for a moment. When I was in high school, I had some free time, so what did I think would be fun to do? Not one of the fun things you were thinking—I decided to do a Bible word study on "humility!" I looked up each word translated *humble* in the Greek and Hebrew and saw how the Bible authors used them.

My nerdy high school quest taught my younger self something, and it can teach us something today as well: humility is a powerful life accelerator. When we acknowledge our need for God, he comes near to us. When we are *not* proud, God is *not* against us. Humility puts us in a right perspective to work with God and others. Humility puts us in a position where we are able to learn from anyone and accept our need for help. Humility helped me realize I was in over my head and needed to accelerate my learning with cassette tapes on my five-hour car ride.

God taught Nebuchadnezzar a lesson we all must learn: we can either humble ourselves, or circumstances will arise that will humble us. I don't know about you, but I will choose to humble myself, thank you very much!

An action often associated with humility creates a good mental picture to live out humility. A humble person in the old days (and sometimes, nowadays) would bow, kneel, or a lay flat before someone. Physical posture shows deference and respect. This gives me an idea for one of our challenge options for today.

THOUGHT FOR THE DAY

Humility is not putting yourself down.
It is maintaining awareness you need of God and others.

CHALLENGE 1

In your prayer time, try something new (or something you haven't done in a while) like bowing, kneeling, or laying before the Lord (but not sleeping!).

CHALLENGE 2

Take some time and create a picture (either in your mind or otherwise) of a powerful God who is ruler of the universe. Try to carry this picture of God in your mind as you go through your day.

CHALLENGE 3

Request some resources from your local library about something you are learning.

BIBLE READING FOR TODAY

Daniel 4

Jot down any impressions you feel God puts on your heart.

Day 8

YOU ARE NOT GOING TO TALK ABOUT GOALS, ARE YOU?

If you have been with me since Day 1 of this book, it should not surprise you that I am a big fan of goals. With accelerated learning and time management for hobbies, it was bound to happen. I even have a goal for how many words of this book I need to write today. So, it also shouldn't surprise you one of my favorite Bible characters is Nehemiah. Let's crank up the old time machine to bring in Nehemiah for a podcast.

In our interview with Nehemiah, we meet the guy who went back and helped lead the rebuilding of the wall around the city of Jerusalem, the holy city of God's people. This was in the days after God's people were tragically exiled into a foreign land. Rebuilding an entire wall would be impressive enough, but the timeframe is even more interesting: 52 days—they built an entire wall around Jerusalem in less than the time it takes to construct a modern single-family home.

Nehemiah shows us three things.

Nehemiah was clear on what needed to be done. It wasn't, "We are going to start rebuilding this wall while we construct a fantastic entertainment destination in the center of the city." It was simply, "We are going to rebuild this wall!" Evangelist

Dwight L. Moody said, "Give me a man who says this one thing I do, and not those fifty things I dabble in."

Nehemiah divided up the work. At first glance Nehemiah 3 seems like a boring list of names in the Bible. On closer glance, the chapter shows us that each person had their assigned task. By dividing and delegating, he kept the work from seeming overwhelming, just like my daily writing goal.

Nehemiah stayed focused on the task. God's enemies did everything in their power to distract Nehemiah. Nehemiah wouldn't get distracted or even meet with these people. This works whether you are working on something as a group or individually. Again, I get more done with this book when I don't get distracted.

> **GOALS GIVE YOU A DIRECTION AND SOMEWHERE TO GO.**

Andy Stanley's great book, *The Principle of the Path: How to Get from Where You Are to Where You Want to Be*, encourages people to wisely choose their path, because when you start on a path, you normally end up wherever the path takes you. This is, in essence, why goals work. Goals give you a direction and somewhere to go. I like the idea by John Maxwell that there are two parts to a decision. There is making a decision, and then there is managing the decision. Both are crucial to success.

Say, for example, you want to eat healthier. First, you must commit fully to pursue this goal. It seems simple, but we have all seen people who really haven't *fully committed* to eat healthier. They start well but stop after a short time. Going back to Maxwell's idea, they *made* the decision, but they didn't *manage* it. Managing the decision to eat healthier is a day-to-day process that affects everything from your grocery list to what you order at the restaurant.

This could apply to any area of life, but I want you to think about those things that God has told you to do with your life. Maybe, he put a dream on your heart when you were young. Maybe, you've had a burden on your heart to start a certain outreach in your neighborhood. Go over these things in your mind.

THOUGHT FOR THE DAY

When we factor God into the equation, most of us should set bigger goals.

Now that you have thought about what God has said to you in the past, choose one of these three challenges.

CHALLENGE 1

Write down a list of things you believe God has told you to do in life that He may still have for you to do. Then, begin to pray and re-examine if God still has these plans for you.

CHALLENGE 2

Send a list of goals you may have already made for the year to the person you are doing this book with, or someone you trust to encourage you in the process.

CHALLENGE 3

Take 15 minutes to write out the steps to complete one of

your goals. Then, take five minutes to do something towards the first step on that goal. Just do *something*.

BIBLE READING FOR TODAY

Proverbs 21:5 (in *The Message* version, if you have it available).

Jot down any impressions you feel God puts on your heart.

Day 9

DO SOMETHING FUN

We've had fun with the time machine motif in this book so far. I really do think a time machine would be great for studying the Bible. It would be nice to at least have a movie presentation of the actual event, to transfer some of the details of the story, like the emotion of how someone is saying something.

At one of the churches I pastored, we did the Philip Yancey video series for his book, *The Jesus I Never Knew*. In the video series, Yancey sampled clips of various Hollywood movies about Jesus and asked how close to reality the movie might have been. One of the things I noticed was that the actors playing Jesus were always very serious. For this reason, I appreciate Bruce Marchiano's less-serious portrayal of Jesus in the video series, *The Book of Matthew*, where we see Jesus smiling and laughing.

I miss the practice and full acceptance of the true joy of Jesus in the church today. Being joyful is not always one of my attributes, so this is a challenge as much for me as for you.

Paul commands us in Philippians 4:4 to "rejoice in the Lord always" (Rejoicing is connected with joy.) Biblical joy is a fruit of the Spirit, so we should experience joy just by spending time with Jesus and in His Word. In the Bible, rest, joy, and fun are almost inseparable. The Old Testament instructions on feasts give us a picture of celebration we shouldn't easily forget. Growing up as one of God's children meant you know how to party, at the right times, of course.

So, when Jesus encourages us to become like children, we can't forget joy. A child like my daughter, Samantha, doesn't struggle to play. Our Lord is the same. We follow a master who used jokes on the Sermon on the Mount and gave his disciples endearing nicknames like "the sons of thunder" (Mark 3:17). And after an intense ministry season, he would pull aside His disciples to rest.

Take, for example, my earthly father, Ted. He is a really fun-loving guy. He's given me great example of joy that has stuck with me for many years. Before he retired, one of the jobs he had required a stressful commute in traffic. My dad decided to make his commute more fun and spread a little joy at the same time by wearing a clown nose as he drove. People would notice my dad, a short Sri Lankan man wearing a clown nose during his daily commute, and it was pretty hard not to smile, at least a little bit!

> **BIBLICAL JOY IS A FRUIT OF THE SPIRIT. WE SHOULD EXPERIENCE JOY WHEN SPENDING TIME WITH JESUS AND IN HIS WORD.**

May we never lose the whimsy and fun of living in Christ, despite life's temporary hardships. Paul's command to the church in Philippi to "rejoice in the Lord always" is a theme embedded throughout the book—and Paul's entire life. We must remember Paul wrote the letter to his church not from a posh apartment or a comfortable retreat but from a prison cell! Paul's life and teachings remind us biblical joy exists independently from our circumstances.

This lesson on suffering would have spoken loud and clear to the church who remembered all too well the story of when God's workers, Paul and Silas, were flogged within an inch of their lives and then thrown, temporarily, into a jail in their very own town. They went through it as a community and knew full well what suffering for Christ looked like.

For today's podcast, let's imagine a conversation with Silas, Paul's companion, as we run our time machine. When you sit down with Silas, you quickly realize you're talking with an interesting person. He shares how he and Paul encouraged each other in that jail cell. His eyes well with tears, and he breaks into a moving hymn he and Paul sang together in their pain and suffering. "Wherever God is, worship breaks out," he says. "Paul picked this song." He then sings another song, noting this was one he picked. You listen to the courage and conviction in this impromptu worship service, and you hear not sadness but pure joy—and a joy clearly not tied to circumstances. "If not for our chains and our wounds, I think we could have danced the night away in that little cell," says Silas. "God is so good!" As he finishes his last song, you wipe a tear from your own eye and are filled with the simple conviction you can face *anything* through God's joy.

THOUGHT FOR THE DAY

Most of us take ourselves too seriously and God not seriously enough.

If you think of your current circumstances as a jail, my challenge is for you to sing there today! But since we have been having some intense challenges, today's challenge is to do something fun.

CHALLENGE 1

Contact a friend who always brings you joy, and if possible, catch up a few minutes today and have a good laugh.

CHALLENGE 2

Set a timer for 30 minutes and goof off. Maybe, watch YouTube videos of silly cats. Maybe, start an epic water fight with your kids. The choice is yours!

CHALLENGE 3

Doing something unexpected can give us joy. Pick a different route to travel if you're out and about. Try a fun, new recipe. Expect to make mistakes and enjoy the process.

BIBLE READING FOR TODAY

"I commend to you the enjoyment of life" (Ecclesiastes 8:15).

Jot down any impressions you feel God puts on your heart.

_____

_____

_____

_____

_____

_____

Day 10

SIMPLICITY AND ORGANIZATION

I grew up in a church that encouraged us to read the Bible every year from Genesis to Revelation. This encouragement always produced good intentions: people would start reading the book of Genesis in January with great enthusiasm. The problems often began in the books after Genesis. It can be difficult to read Exodus, Leviticus, and Numbers, which share Israel's family history, along with God's blueprint for the new society, called the Law.

Let's get deeper insight on these famously challenging books by interviewing a Hebrew priest from Bible times. As the priest comes in and sits down, you notice right away his confusion. Even more than other interviewees, he seems shocked by the microphones and cords. He begins to ask about how they all work. After a while, you realize that part of his interest in these things is because he was in charge of communication for the Israelites in the desert.

After fascinatedly playing with the microphone for a few minutes, the priest explains that communication is not very easy for his people. They have had to find different ways to let people know what to do and what God wants them to do next. To do this, they communicate with musical instruments, specifically trumpets.

The trumpets tell the people what to do next. If both the trumpets sound together, everyone knows to gather for a meeting. Another type of trumpet blast tells the people which "tribes" (*tribes* meaning populous clans of people descended from the sons of Jacob) should begin to move out. As the priest describes his job, it reminds you of a traffic cop. The priest's job is to guide and direct the people. He prevents complete chaos.

When we read the books of the Law, we forget how this large community wandering in the desert could easily have devolved into chaos and disorder. They didn't know how to operate as a nation, yet they became one the day they walked out of Egypt. One of God's characteristics is to bring order out of chaos.

Just as he took a formless world and brought order to it in the biblical creation account (Genesis 1–2), God took Abraham's little family and built a nation out of it. As the priest gets in the time machine to get back to work directing traffic for the community of Israel, his story reminds you of the beauty in something as simple as a trumpet blast. God was helping this new nation to function in a simple way to accomplish its purpose.

My wife and I chose as a family song the old Shaker tune, "Simple Gifts." The first line is important to us: "Tis a gift to be simple, tis a gift to be free." We have come to find the truth of those words. It really is a gift of God to live in simplicity. Another family phrase we have adopted is, "Simplicity isn't simple." But it *is* a great way to live and one of our family values.

To find simplicity, we have to embrace other words like "margin," "organization," and "enough." God wants a restful, orderly life for us, and it doesn't happen by accident. Making margin is when we leave room in our resources. It is a beautiful place and lifestyle that allows a person to jump on the adventures that Jesus calls us to take with Him. Organization creates the structure where margin is possible, and *enough* is a choice to say no when outside things try to invade our margin.

Living simply requires us to make tough choices. The world pushes us to a life of increasing complexity, but we must challenge the definition of success by living for more than "keeping up with the Joneses." This is where Holy Spirit's creativity comes into play. Walking with the Spirit starts with obedience. By

> **GOD WANTS A RESTFUL, ORDERLY LIFE FOR US, AND IT DOESN'T HAPPEN BY ACCIDENT.**

listening to God, we each become a canvas on which God can paint His picture. In future days in this book, we will look at the ideas of organization and enough, but let's get started by creating some margin so we can take on the adventures God has for us.

While creating margin can be difficult, it can also bring new freedom. Most of us understand the concept of margin. If you have margin in your budget, it means you spend less than what comes in each month.

Margin doesn't care how much or how little you make. You can make a million dollars a month, but if you spend it all, you still have no margin. On the other hand, you could leave a portion of a modest income each month and achieve margin.

The concept of margin also applies to our time, money, and emotional health. In a world that glorifies busyness, we must actively avoid traps that rob our margin. We must guard these areas just as we do our financial margin. To keep emotional margin, we must understand what depletes and fills us emotionally. Then, we must work to keep "our tank" full.

Simplicity and Organization

You can either *cut* or *add* to gain margin. If you have no financial margin, you can either *cut* your expenses or *add* to your income. You can use this trick in other areas of your life as well. Time is a limited resource, so we gain most of our margin by cutting. Author Bob Goff, a successful attorney and author who is involved in relief efforts on a global scale, is known for saying he quits something every Thursday—all to preserve his margin.

You can also increase your time margin by using systems and tools to multiply your efforts. For example, by writing this book, I am able to share these ideas with many people without having to sit down with each person personally (although individual ministry to pastors is still a vital part of my ministry, I am limited in the number of people I can personally reach each year).

> **IN A WORLD THAT GLORIFIES BUSYNESS, WE MUST ACTIVELY AVOID TRAPS THAT ROB OUR MARGIN.**

Simplicity is the goal, and organization and margin don't happen by accident. As you wrap up your interview, and the priest gets ready to head back to his people, you ask one more question. "What do all of these systems, rules, and structures do for your people?" He answers, "Oh that is easy. It gives us a framework to experience God." With that thought running through your mind, you decide to embrace simplicity for yourself.

THOUGHT FOR THE DAY

Simplicity gives us a framework to experience God.

CHALLENGE 1

Create more margin by canceling something that no longer

gives you value, like TV service, a magazine subscription, or newspaper delivery. If you don't subscribe to traditional media, try deleting an app from your mobile device that takes time that you no longer want to give it.

CHALLENGE 2

Quit something. This may be a work group that no longer serves a purpose, or a social group it is time to let go of for the next season of your life.

CHALLENGE 3

Set a timer for 30 minutes and unsubscribe or turn off emails or other notifications that no longer add value for you. Again, remember this is to open up space for the new things that God might want to add to your life.

BIBLE READING FOR TODAY

Numbers 10:1–10. Imagine your new friend, the priest, blowing the trumpets.

Jot down any impressions you feel God puts on your heart.

_____
_____
_____
_____
_____

Day 11

ORDER OUT OF CHAOS

After visiting yesterday with the priest, you are ready to meet with another person from that time period: Elizur, son of Shedeur, of the tribe of Reuben. You can't find out much about this man, so you are curious why your time machine is bringing him to the podcast.

As you both sit down and the recording gets going, you ask some basic questions about Elizur's life. He lived in the time of Moses and was a chief in the tribe of Reuben. Knowing that, you ask about all of the stories of dramatic events that happened during that time. This creates some interesting stories, but you have a feeling there is more to learn from Elizur.

It is when you ask about his role as a chief that you begin to understand why he is here today. When the trumpets go off (remember their purpose from yesterday), it is Elizur's job to lead the tribe to wherever they are heading. He lets you know there's an order to how the tribes went out, and there's an order to how they camp around the tabernacle when they aren't moving.

Elizur explains to you the genius of this arrangement. If someone ever gets separated from the tribe when they are on the move, the order helps them reunite with their family. Parents, for example, can use their position in relationship to the tabernacle to help kids find things or find their way home.

Elizur confirms what the priest taught you yesterday: God is bringing order out of the chaos that the nation of Israel brought from the day they walked out of Egypt. Each instruction from God helps build a framework for the country to function more effectively. This framework helps them perform their purpose in the world. A helpful way for me to think about organization is comparing it to the metal frame that holds up a building. The structure allows all of the other activity to happen in a building. The same can be true of our lives.

This understanding also helps release us from guilt and unneeded pressure. I have read books that make a person feel like they are a failure if one drawer in their house is a mess. Let's put this in perspective. The structure of our lives provides the strength we need to fulfill the purpose God, the master Creator, has for us in the world. We *do* need enough structure and organization to live in obedience to the plans that God has for our lives. We work through this together with God.

Without organization, some people are not able to complete the mission God has for their lives. They can't visit a friend in need because they can't even find their car keys. More structure in some people's lives would allow them the freedom they need to eliminate distractions from more important

> **THE STRUCTURE OF OUR LIVES PROVIDES THE STRENGTH WE NEED TO FULFILL THE PURPOSE GOD HAS FOR US IN THE WORLD.**

things. This said, the flip side can also be true. Structure can become a cage that holds us in rather than sets us free. Our lives become so "organized" there is no flexibility and freedom to capture moments with God.

As Elizur ends the interview, you are left with nagging questions: Which side of the spectrum do I most lean toward?

Where do I need more structure, and where do I need more freedom? Will I let God challenge me with how my life could be different?

THOUGHT FOR THE DAY

Structure and organization can help us live in obedience to the plans that God has for our lives.

CHALLENGE 1

If you need more organization in your life, don't try to reorganize your whole life. Find one small thing that brings stress, like your bed stand, and start with that simple project today.

CHALLENGE 2

If you need less structure in your life, think of one organizational obligation you can skip today. Maybe, you were planning on working on a non-vital house project tonight. Take the time and play with your kids instead.

CHALLENGE 3

Take 15–20 minutes, with a timer, and think through the organization and structure of one area of your life. What is working and what is not working? Write down how it could be different.

BIBLE READING FOR TODAY

Matthew 25:14–30, a reminder of the importance of taking care of the life we have been given.

Jot down any impressions you feel God puts on your heart.

Day 12

ENOUGH

You begin to wonder if the time machine is broken or stuck. For the third day in a row, the person you interview is from the time period when the Israelites were in the desert after leaving Egypt. After you verify that the machine is working by checking the onboard diagnostics, you start up the machine, and two cranky ladies come out.

Both ladies seem a little agitated about something. One lady walks back and forth around the room pacing, and the other sits in a chair just shaking her head. The seated lady introduces herself as Sarah. She says she was named after her ancestor, but that she doesn't feel much like her today. She says the other lady's name is Rebecca. Rebecca is still pacing and muttering.

When you finally get them set up for the interview, you are ready to get them talking. Sometimes you are concerned if you will be able to get your guests to open up, but this is not one of those times. All you have to do is ask the question, "What just happened?" They both start wildly telling their story, jumping over each other's sentences.

Slowing them down, Rebecca says, "The place just smelt!!"

"And those wormy, maggoty things!" says Sarah.

"What wormy, maggoty things?" you ask. They tell you it all began when the two of them were talking while getting water.

Sarah had been talking about how she was tired of collecting the manna every day. Rebecca mentioned that she thought it would be nice to wake up in the morning and just have some sitting there for the cooking.

As a good interviewer, you don't assume your listeners are familiar with manna, so you ask them to tell the backstory (Exodus 16). Sarah shares how as the Israelites left Egypt and crossed the Red Sea, they needed to have food for so many people. God promised to take care of them. The next morning, white, flaky stuff covered the ground. Moses, their leader, told the people to pick it up and eat it.

The two friends had loved the challenge of coming up with different ways to make it every day. When someone in the camp invented a new recipe, word spread like wildfire. Yet, every morning they went out to get more, until today. After their meeting at the water, they agreed to collect more manna than they needed and save it for the next day. They figured it would make their morning a little easier. They both went to sleep feeling pretty proud of themselves.

For Sarah the morning began with the smell. Or even more accurately it began with her son waking her up complaining about the smell. As she went toward the source of the smell, she saw that the manna had gone bad.

Rebecca was a little more freaked out. She hated bugs. Even when she was a little girl, her brothers would creep her out by throwing insects at her. Now, when she looked at her leftover manna, she was thrown into a tailspin because of the creepy crawlers in the manna. You can relate to this, having once left food in your refrigerator over vacation, and you wisely let the ladies get on their way back to their time and place.

The story of the manna teaches us a lot of things, but in listening to these ladies, we are reminded of the lesson of the word "enough." God wants His people to learn to trust Him. Each day is a new lesson in trusting His provision. God wants us to trust Him today, but how do we do that while still taking advantage of a refrigerator that allows us to keep more than one day's worth of food?

Part of an understanding of *enough* is to stop comparing ourselves with other people. If we get our feeling of "enoughness" by comparing ourselves with other people, we will never feel like we are enough. Hip-hop artist and Christ follower Lecrae Moore tells a story that highlights this point. Lecrae attended an exclusive party with all sorts of people near the top of the music industry. What he noticed is that people at the highest level were all still comparing themselves with each other.[1]

> **WE FIND OUR ENOUGH BY BEING OBEDIENT TO THE SPECIFIC ASSIGNMENTS BASED ON THE ROLE GOD HAS FOR US.**

A second part of understanding *enough* is to become clear on what obedience looks like for us. Even in the simple challenges of the day, we find our enough by being obedient to our specific assignments based on the role God has for us. Our obedience to God will look different if we are called to be a business person, a stay at home parent or the pastor of a church. We are doing enough if we complete our assignment not by doing what someone else is supposed to be doing.

A final challenge in learning to live in a place of *enough* is to take a simple step to put yourself in a place of trust, like the Israelites, who trusted God to provide for each day.

THOUGHT FOR THE DAY

*Living with God's "enough" for us
frees us from the need to be someone else.*

God may not call you to a diet of manna, but here are three challenges to try.

CHALLENGE 1

Think of something you keep just to make a statement to other people. Donate it to a charity or friend. Enjoy the new freedom it brings.

CHALLENGE 2

Set a timer for 20 minutes and write a list of specific assignments that God has given to you. This will help you know what obedience looks like.

CHALLENGE 3

Take a step of faith and act on an insight that God has given you while you've been reading this book. We have already covered a lot of ground. Maybe, you need to finish a challenge from a previous day. It is "enough" to go back and finish that challenge.

Enough

BIBLE READING FOR TODAY

Exodus 16

Jot down any impressions you feel God puts on your heart.

Day 13

ADVISORS

Today, as the time machine screeches to a halt, the doors open and release a puff of dust. Out walks a man dressed in fine clothes and wearing an ornate crown. He introduces himself as Rehoboam, King of Israel. You know from your research he is not one of Israel's most famous kings, but you hope to learn great lessons from this "head of state" you will interview.

King Rehoboam has a, "What just hit me?" look on his face. Knowing the story, you can only imagine he has had that look on his face for a long time. King Rehoboam, the son of Solomon, shares some of the blame for Israel's deterioration into civil war (1 Kings 12).

Rehoboam, sitting on your couch with his face in his hands, is muttering to himself, "Why didn't I listen to them?" He looks up at you and says, "I really made a mess of things!" He tells you how, after taking over for his father, he tried to establish himself as king. He was choosing between taking advice from two groups of people: his father's advisors and his own friends. He shakes his head and he wonders again why he took the bad advice of his buddies over the wise advice of the people with perspective.

As you end the interview, you realize how taking good (or bad) advice can profoundly influence a person and even a nation.

Rehoboam's interview ends awkwardly as he remembers he had a hair and skin treatment appointment with his personal stylist.

The Bible gives us stories of many people like Rehoboam who took advice from mentors or advisors. Not all examples turned out so poorly. Jethro spoke wisdom into Moses' life (Exodus 18), Moses poured into Joshua (Exodus 17:14, 24:12–13), and Elijah impacted Elisha (1 Kings 19:19–21.) Elisha later influenced an entire team of prophets. Can you think of others? How about Jesus and the disciples?

One of my favorite ways to learn is from advisors and mentors. God has blessed me with amazing people who have poured into me. No matter where you are in life, you can go even further when others invest in you. Here are five tips to find a mentor or mentors.

Don't be afraid to ask. I learned years ago that it never hurts to ask someone to mentor or advise you. The worst that can happen is they might say no, but they also might say yes. I've heard it said to ask the most unlikely person that you can and you might just get a yes since not a lot of people ask them. So it begins with the Ask.

> **NO MATTER WHERE YOU ARE IN LIFE, YOU CAN GO EVEN FURTHER WHEN OTHERS INVEST IN YOU.**

Get a group of advisors rather than a lone guru on a hill. I find that it is helpful for me to have a group of people that I can ask for help rather than one person. I get different perspectives, and that is helpful with difficult problems. It also takes the pressure off one person to be "Mr. or Mrs. Answer Person."

Be willing to go at the pace they are able to go with you. Some mentors are able to meet on a regular basis, and others are able to meet less frequently. Some may prefer email, while others may prefer the phone or in person. Staying flexible allows you to grow even if these individuals don't have a lot of time to give.

Seek out specific advisors for specific problems. Some mentors or advisors may come alongside you for a specific issue you are dealing with in life. For example, I seek out certain people for advice on car issues; others give input in other areas. Each person has a skill in an area I need. Maybe, you are working on a specific business problem you could share with someone a few steps ahead. Is there a person in your church who has the type of marriage you want, who you would love to learn from?

Take action on the advice of your mentors. It might take time to implement all the advice, but start somewhere and take action right away. If someone gives you good advice, and you do nothing with it, eventually, the advice stops coming. Finding some specific item that you can put into action will give you great momentum.

THOUGHT FOR THE DAY

We might be one piece of advice away from our next breakthrough.

Building an "advisory council" takes time, but we don't want that to stand in the way of taking action today.

CHALLENGE 1

Think of one person you admire personally, professionally, or spiritually. Before the day is over, reach out to them. Maybe, you can contact them with a very specific question that they could help you with very quickly.

CHALLENGE 2

Think of any advice someone gave you that you still need to implement. Take a step on it today. Then, if possible, send the person a thank-you note.

CHALLENGE 3

Think about some of the areas of your life you struggle with right now. What are some key questions you need answered? Pick one and then brainstorm some people who could help you in that area. Remember, you can learn from people through books, videos, etc., not just in person.

BIBLE READING FOR TODAY

1 Kings 12:1–19: "a king who didn't listen to advice"

Jot down any impressions you feel God puts on your heart.

_____
_____
_____
_____
_____
_____
_____
_____
_____

Day 14

INVEST IN OTHERS

Yesterday, we looked at one side of the mentor and advisor relationship: getting mentorship. But that's only half the fun. Let's talk about giving back through mentorship. One of my dad's favorite verses is, "And the things you have heard me say in the presence of many witnesses entrust to reliable men who will also be qualified to teach others" (2 Timothy 2:2). Mentorship is like a pipeline of passing along the goodness of God.

Imagine with me for a moment you are Timothy, a young minister in the 1st-century church. Paul has picked you as one of the people he is going to pour his life into. You spend time together, and you get to see him minister to God's people and go through everyday life. You know his morning routine, how he likes his dinner, how he's always praying through the highs and lows of his ministry. You do life together. So, when Paul writes you a letter telling you that the chain shouldn't stop with you, your goal is to find people to pour into who will be able to pour into others, just like Paul did for you.

This is one of the great missed opportunities I see in the church today. People sit Sunday after Sunday in a service and miss out on the joy of investing in others. You might be thinking, "I don't have it together enough to invest in someone," or "It

Invest in Others

would be weird for me to go up to someone and say I want to be their mentor." Let's look at these one at a time.

"I don't have it together enough to invest in someone." Yesterday, you reached out to someone to ask them to invest in you. I can guarantee that they do not have it all together. As you get to know them and your group of advisors better, you will realize that every one of them have areas where they want to grow. I was meeting with an advisor who leads an organization reaching people around the globe. He shared with me the desire to be better at personal evangelism. High school students can be mentors for junior high students. So if you are waiting till you have it all together, you'll never start.

> **PEOPLE SIT SUNDAY AFTER SUNDAY IN A SERVICE AND MISS OUT ON THE JOY OF INVESTING IN OTHERS.**

"It would be weird for me to go up to someone and say I want to be their mentor." You are right, that would be weird. As you look at people to pour your life into, you may never start a conversation saying, "I want to mentor you." Mentorship begins with building a relationship. Yes, sometimes it is structured like when you lead a small group, but often it is much more informal. You may meet for coffee every few months. You may pray together at the prayer meeting. One of my mentors just encourages people to begin to pray for God to connect them with someone who they can mentor and see what God does.

THOUGHT FOR THE DAY

Your greatest accomplishments in life may come through the people in whom you invest.

CHALLENGE 1

If no one comes to mind you can invest in, take at least 10 minutes today and ask God to show you someone. Even if they are not in your life now, pray that God would bring people into your life.

CHALLENGE 2

One place to start investing in others is through encouragement. Reach out to someone and call out a positive quality you see in them. Encourage them that you believe in them.

CHALLENGE 3

Maybe, today is a reminder of a person you started to invest in but need to take it to the next level. Reach out to them and let them know that you would like to connect to catch up or hear their story.

BIBLE READING FOR TODAY

Matthew 28:16–20

Jot down any impressions you feel God puts on your heart.

_____
_____
_____
_____
_____

Day 15

GET A PASSPORT

Abraham is admiring your furniture. Yes, the one and only Abraham, the father of many nations! One of the most famous people of all time is sitting in your living room.

You're a little star struck as Abraham tells you about how God challenged him to leave his home and go to a place God would show him. Abraham's story challenges and reminds you of God's promise that, with obedience, Abraham would be a blessing to many nations.

As Abraham shares the story of his journey, you follow along with a map on your phone. The geography today has cities and some level of human infrastructure, but you realize the Holy Land of ancient times had none of these things. Abraham couldn't check his favorite travel site for the best place for him to stay at the next town. He did not have the option of viewing with a few clicks a video of the place he was about to arrive at the next day. Travel in the wilderness was rugged, unknown, and actually dangerous. But at the same time, Abraham shared how the nations would be blessed because he obeyed.

With this story in mind, I have a confession to make. I am a missionary kid. Living part of my childhood in Sri Lanka has forever changed the way that I look at the world. Like Abraham, travel is part of my story. During seasons of less travel, it is sometimes hard for me when I don't know the next time I am going to board a plane.

We live in a connected world that allows our heart to be impacted by the adventure of the worldwide family of God. Abraham's interview reminds us that God continues to call us outside of our comfort zone to make an impact to people who are not like us. That's also one message of the book of Acts, how God pushes people outside of their comfort zones.

It is easy for those of us in a western culture to create a bubble that keeps us from touching the world outside. Yet, God is still in the business of calling people beyond their comfort zone. And in a country where immigration brings many people and cultures to our doorstep, that may mean our neighbors across the street.

Sensing your own hesitancy to touch the world and other cultures that seem so scary and different, you ask Abraham how he did it. He shares that he had in his mind a city he was headed to that was planned and built by God. He moved outside his comfort zone ethnically and culturally because his vision for his life was longer than this life offered.

> **GOD IS STILL IN THE BUSINESS OF CALLING PEOPLE BEYOND THEIR COMFORT ZONE.**

Abraham reminds us of what we have been learning all along here. If we are going to live the adventure that God has for our lives, we will need to see and live beyond today.

THOUGHT FOR THE DAY

Our vision of the future pushes us to move outside the creature comforts of today.

For some of us, this nudge of heaven may take us to locations and people we never thought, but we can't let our "someday" keep us from experiencing God expanding our heart today.

CHALLENGE 1

If you live in a place with an ethnic restaurant you haven't tried, check it out today. As you dine, maybe as a family, pray for the country of origin of the restaurant owners and ask how you might be a blessing to your neighbors.

CHALLENGE 2

Commit to learning another language. In today's world, it is easier than ever to begin learning a language. And there *is* an app for that.

CHALLENGE 3

Sign up for a mission trip through your church or another missions organization. You may not need to go halfway around the world. Most major cities have outreaches to ethnic groups you could join with little cost or time commitment.

BIBLE READING FOR TODAY

Mark 16:15–18

Jot down any impressions you feel God puts on your heart.

Day 16

SPEAK WISELY

When the time machine starts to work today, you can feel your heart beating a little faster. Today, you are going to be interviewing none other than Nathan the prophet. This is the guy who went to King David and exposed his adultery and murder (2 Samuel 12). You hope that this interview doesn't turn into a prophetically inspired conversation about any sin in your life!

When Nathan steps into your living room, he's not the fire-and-brimstone prophet you expected. He seems like a very thoughtful person who is genuinely interested in you. When he asks a question about a family picture on the wall, you begin to relax.

As Nathan tells the story of his encounter with David, you begin to see another side of the story. What was it like to be Nathan in that situation? You can imagine if God had shown you these facts and wanted you to go and confront David. Nathan was aware of what David was capable of doing. On more than one occasion, people had brought information into David's court and didn't live to tell about it.

> **OUR WORDS CAN MEAN LIFE OR DEATH TO PEOPLE.**

Nathan explains how he figured out a plan. Rather than immediately telling David he is a sinner, Nathan starts with a story, to get David's heart in a position to receive the incoming message. The takeaway? Words have power—we choose not just what we say but how we say it. Being gracious and thoughtful can help our words have greater impact.

Sometimes, our words can mean life or death to people. Even when God gives us challenging words, Nathan's story reminds us humility and wisdom can keep these words from doing damage. Much of our journey with Jesus will take us to messy, uncomfortable places with people. We are going to make mistakes, and some people are going to treat us wrongly, whether intentional or not.

THOUGHT FOR THE DAY

*Being gracious and thoughtful
can help our words have greater impact.*

My challenge for you today is not to go and show someone their sin. I do want you to think about how you can become good at two specific skills.

Improving conversations. This includes making good conversations great, not just difficult conversations better.

Taking time to process when God speaks to you. Learning to humbly share an impression from God is part of the adventure of following Jesus. Most of the time, this is an encouragement to a person and not correction. Mastering this skill begins with knowing how to capture the things you feel God is saying to you.

Speak Wisely

CHALLENGE 1

Think of one way to improve your conversation today. Even if it is just hanging out with a friend for lunch, what is something you could say to encourage that person today?

CHALLENGE 2

Nathan brought creativity into his interactions. How can you approach one of your tasks today with this same wisdom? For example, if you are a stay-at-home parent, what is one way to inject a little more creativity to something you have planned with your kids today?

CHALLENGE 3

In this book, we've provided a space each day for you to record the impressions God is putting on your heart. Take a moment to work out a plan to capture those thoughts when this book is done. Think both digital and paper. Maybe, your challenge for today is to find notebook or open a document to organize and save these thoughts.

BIBLE READING FOR TODAY

2 Samuel 12:1–14

Jot down any impressions you feel God puts on your heart.

_____

_____

Day 17

SHUT IT OFF

Today, when the time machine comes to a stop, the door opens, and no one is there. On the floor of the time machine is a note:

> *No one is coming today. Enjoy some solitude.*
> *~ Kevin*

Solitude? This could be interesting.

Solitude does not always get good press. People fear loneliness. For example, when you want to punish someone in prison, you send them to "solitary" confinement. Yet, the Bible tells us, "Jesus often withdrew to lonely places and prayed" (Luke 5:16). This said, finding the time and space to be alone can be a challenge for many of us.

I'm writing today from a place of solitude so I can focus on this book. Without Wi-Fi, Netflix, or cable, it amazes me how much time I can find for reading, writing, and prayer. I am reminded of the words of Richard Foster, that solitude helps us "resign as CEO of the universe".[2] We might fear we're missing out, but Jesus and others showed us what to do in solitude: pray.

I have found two important things about being alone.

In being alone we have more space to listen. Moses was on the mountain with God, and God spoke to him. The words he heard on that mountain are things we still read today in the Bible. I am not suggesting that, if you set aside some time of solitude, God is going to give you the next Ten Commandments, but you *will* have greater space to hear, which could have a big impact on your life.

In being alone we give up control which was never really ours. As Richard Foster has reminded us, it is important to remember that the position of CEO of the universe is already taken. No matter how many tweets, status updates, and text messages we make, this fact is not going to change. Reminding ourselves we are not the boss can be powerful and freeing.

> **WE MIGHT FEAR WE ARE MISSING OUT, BUT JESUS AND OTHERS SHOWED US WHAT TO DO IN SOLITUDE: PRAY.**

Maybe, my challenge should be for you to leave this moment and head for the highest mountain you can find to go and be alone with God. For most of you, that would be impossible. It does not mean that we cannot reap the benefits of solitude. Brother Lawrence, who worked in a kitchen, would enter his solitude in the midst of his cleaning. John and Charles Wesley's mother would put a cloth over her head as she sat in a chair and prayed as a sign to the kids that she was not to be disturbed.

THOUGHT FOR THE DAY

Solitude helps us resign as CEO of the universe.
~ Richard Foster

Our time machine will be back to its normal self tomorrow, but today let's try and experiment with something that many of the people we interview practiced. Today's challenge is to spend 30 minutes in solitude.

CHALLENGE 1

If you work in an office, take a walk for your lunch, leaving the office and your cell phone behind. Simply be alone with God.

CHALLENGE 2

Find your 30 minutes of solitude this evening by turning off the television or Internet (and all other devices) thirty minutes before going to sleep.

CHALLENGE 3

If neither Challenge 1 nor 2 works for you, simply take some time today and read over the notes you have jotted up to this point and see if you notice any patterns. Focus on what you are reading while you are doing it.

BIBLE READING FOR TODAY

Luke 5:12–16

Jot down any impressions you feel God puts on your heart.

_____

_____

_____

Day 18

GIVE SOMETHING AWAY

Today's interviewee is a surprise. He's an older gentleman still a little surprised to be a part of your podcast. "I was just telling a story to my grandchildren when all of a sudden I showed up here!" he says in bewilderment.

When you tell the man you are a follower of Christ and are doing a Bible interview podcast, he says, "Jesus? I met him when I was just a little kid!" He had heard stories of Jesus, so he went out to hear him speak. He was definitely not disappointed.

Jesus could teach like no one he had ever heard before or since. When it came time for lunch, he willingly gave up his lunch, and Jesus miraculously multiplied the bread and fishes to feed 5000 people (Matthew 14:13–21)! That man probably ate a lot of meals after that day, but none would compare to the one that he gave away.

Most of us don't know the stories we'll tell our grandchildren. Or even better, we don't know the stories that are going to follow us to heaven. "This is the lady who . . ."

"Remember the guy that Jesus was talking about, this is that guy . . ."

Yet, at the time, it may feel like we are giving our lunch away, without knowing how we'll eat that day. We can let go, and not out of guilt but out of what we might gain. We hold on to a lot of things that will seem unimportant in the few moments when we pass into eternity.

The Bible is filled with stories of people glad they gave things away. You may have even heard the saying, "You can't out give God." I have found this to be true my entire life, even as a child.

Giving can feel scary, maybe the little boy felt this way giving away his food for the day. But while we lose a feeling of control when we give, we gain a greater ability to trust God. Our giving can bless one person or even thousands, like the little boy's lunch donation. What's more, giving can create stories that last a lifetime.

> **WE HOLD ON TO A LOT OF THINGS THAT WILL SEEM UNIMPORTANT WHEN WE PASS INTO ETERNITY.**

THOUGHT FOR THE DAY

We never know how our generosity will be the story people talk about in heaven.

My challenges for you are very straightforward today. Give something away. It doesn't have to be big. Maybe, it just feels like five loaves and two fish. Be obedient to whatever it is that God challenges you to do. The goal is to do something today. What will you give to Jesus?

CHALLENGE 1

Do you have a donation center like the Salvation Army in your area? Look around your house. Is there something that you could donate today? It may not be something you were even

Give Something Away

planning on giving away. But now as you pray, maybe this item comes to mind, and you can even drop it off today.

CHALLENGE 2

Do you have something that would bless a friend or neighbor? As you think of this item and this person, you may sense they would love to receive it as a gift from you. If you feel that God would have you give this, try to find a way to give it to them today.

CHALLENGE 3

The key to these challenges is the actions that you take. Just reading them will only do so much good. So if your circumstances don't allow you to give something away today, I don't want that to keep you from the adventure of following Jesus. If you can't do one of the first two items, give a donation online. Think of one of your favorite charities, churches, or ministries and give them something today.

BIBLE READING FOR TODAY

John 6:1–13

Jot down any impressions you feel God puts on your heart.

_____
_____
_____
_____

Day 19

PRAY FOR SOMEONE

You're running behind today. It's yet another reminder you can increase margin in your life by letting go of things that aren't eternally important. Today, you will be interviewing James, who wrote the book of the Bible named after him. Before you sit down at the microphone, you take a quick picture together to keep for your scrapbook. James mentions how some people thought he looked like his dad, Joseph, and some thought he looked more like his mother Mary. That's right. James is the half-brother of Jesus Christ.

James quickly puts life in perspective. He paints a picture of what it was like to have Jesus for a brother. Imagine your mother asking you, "Why can't you be more like your older brother, Jesus?" But he explains how he and his other brothers would make fun of Jesus at times in His ministry. This considered, James is amazed the early church made him a leader. It is also easy to see why James wrote on the importance of taming your tongue (James 3:3–12).

James reminds us our words have power. *Your* words have power. The writer of Proverbs reminds us the tongue has the power of life and death (18:21). Proverbs also says, "Gracious words are a honeycomb, sweet to the soul and healing to the bones" (16:24). What you say to people, whether by person, phone, email, or even text, can encourage them. To paraphrase Dr. David Jeremiah, "Encouragement is speaking truth to people's fears." You can speak life to people.

But where do these words of life come from? You decide to ask James. He tells you what his brother, Jesus, said: our heart is the place where our words originate (Matt 12:34). This means our inner life determines, in large part, our ability to speak life into others.

Many encouraging words come from constantly feeding on God's word in the Bible. We must also remember the still, small voice is where we get laser-like precision to speak to people's fears. God speaks to your heart so you can speak to the heart of others.

When asking God to give me the right words for the right people, I have been amazed again and again how a phrase God throws into my head before or during a conversation is just the right word for that person. The key is to be willing to listen to God so that I have the words to speak. Are you willing to spend time in prayer, listening, so that you can bring words of life to a friend in need?

> **GOD SPEAKS TO YOUR HEART SO YOU CAN SPEAK TO THE HEART OF OTHERS.**

Praying for someone is one of the greatest gifts that you can give to them. The difference that you can make in the life of others is amazing. But we have to take action. Many of us tell people we will pray for them but never get around to doing it. So I recommend to people that if someone asks you to pray for them, do it right then.

God may impress on your heart someone to pray for specifically. The other day, I was talking on the phone with a friend who was going through a hard time. I periodically update my 3x5 index cards that I carry with me as reminders for prayer (for more info on that check out my book, *Enjoying Prayer*). I told my friend that for the next six months, I would add him to the card I pray through each Monday. Knowing that I would be putting my friend's name on the card, I knew I wouldn't forget to pray for him. These prayers for this friend over the next six months are going to make a difference for the rest of his life.

You can give that gift to someone else as well. Like the man we talked to with the loaves and fish, your prayer can have a multiplied effect on people's lives. If it is a day or week or month or year, your prayer can be like a slow investment in a bank account that compounds with interest.

THOUGHT FOR THE DAY

Your words and prayer for others are like gifts that can last a lifetime.

CHALLENGE 1

Pick one of the missionaries of your church. Pray for them. Then, send them a message and let them know some of the things that you prayed for them today.

CHALLENGE 2

Think of someone that you know is going through a hard time. Pray for them. Then, send them a message letting them know what you prayed for them.

CHALLENGE 3

In person, on the phone, or in some other way, speak encouragement and life to some fear a person you know is dealing with at the moment.

BIBLE READING FOR TODAY

James 3:3–12

Jot down any impressions you feel God puts on your heart.

Day 20

FIND YOUR TRUE SOURCE

I love the story of God using ravens to feed Elijah. It shows God's creativity and sense of humor. God decided to take care of Elijah in a way he didn't expect. This story reminds us that God is our ultimate source of provision. Though we may earn an income, God is the reason we are able to work. We are ultimately dependent on Him.

Sometimes, it is easy to think of ourselves as the source of our provision. Maybe, we look at pastors and ministry leaders and think of them depending on God to take care of them. We, however, just "get up and go to work in the morning." This could all change in a moment. Your employer may be bought out. You may get a new boss who doesn't like you that much. If you own a company, in a moment, your industry could radically change due to technology. It is important to remind ourselves that God is the one who provides for our needs.

> **THOUGH WE MAY EARN AN INCOME, GOD IS THE REASON WE ARE ABLE TO WORK.**

Jesus taught his disciples to pray, "Give us this day our daily bread." This verse is a great reminder that we daily need God to take care of us, and we might be surprised how he does it. The first day that Elijah had birds feed him must have been a little strange. The first day that the

Israelites saw manna, it would have been a little surprising. Will you just ask God to do something for you today? I pray you enjoy the way that He surprises you!

THOUGHT FOR THE DAY

*Be daring enough to not put God in a box
when it comes to answering your prayer.*

CHALLENGE 1

Pray that, at some point today, God would show you some way that He is taking care of you. Don't put God in a box of what this should look like. Be a detective looking for clues of His provision.

CHALLENGE 2

Make a list of 15 things that you are thankful that God has provided for you in your life. Highlight two or three that were things that you would not have expected.

CHALLENGE 3

Tell someone a story about a time in your life that God took care of you. Tell them the details you haven't told in a while. Be mindful of the thankfulness you have for God.

BIBLE READING FOR TODAY

1 Kings 17

Jot down any impressions you feel God puts on your heart.

Day 21

DO SOMETHING EXTRA FOR THE MINISTRY YOU SERVE

One of my first jobs was as a Wal-Mart "associate." Early in my training, they told us that when someone asked us where something was in the store, we had to take them to the spot of the item they wanted. I don't know if that is still the policy, but they were trying to teach us good customer service.

It's said that Jack Welch, legendary CEO of General Electric, was asked by an audience member about advice for someone starting out in the business world. His advice was to get out from the heap. Somehow, get out of the pile in order to stand out. The little extra you could do would make all the difference and help you to be noticed by the boss.

What if we were to take these principles and apply them to our walk with Jesus? A great person to interview for your podcast about this principle would be Stephen. Stephen is most known for being the church's first martyr, but his story doesn't start there. He started out with the assignment to wait on tables. It was not a fancy job to take care of dishes and make sure widows did not get neglected.

Somewhere along the line, Stephen didn't stop there. It said that Stephen "did great wonders and miraculous signs among the people" (Acts 6:8). Maybe, one day a widow needed healing, and Stephen didn't wait till the Apostles came around. Whatever the case, Stephen did his ministry assignment plus some. That led to him being used in other ways that would go down in history.

God has called all of us to be a "plus some" kind of people. Paul says it this way: "Whatever you do, work at it with all your heart, as working for the Lord, not for men since you will receive an inheritance from the Lord as a reward. It is the Lord Christ that you are serving" (Colossians 3:23–24).

Whatever you do? Does that include your ministry in the nursery on Sunday? Whatever you do? How about the dead-end job that seems to serve no redeeming value for mankind? My first real job was at a junk mail factory, so I know what that is like. And I am sorry if you got one of our mailings.

The life of a mom is a great example of this principle. If an adult looks back on their childhood with fondness, it is often the little things they remember. My mother made me a stuffed Bert and Ernie when I got chicken pox as a kid. The "plus some" moments make the greatest difference.

> **GOD HAS CALLED ALL OF US TO BE A "PLUS SOME" KIND OF PEOPLE.**

THOUGHT FOR THE DAY

Give a little extra effort today as if you were giving it to Jesus.

CHALLENGE 1

Do a little something extra for a ministry or area you serve in your church. Remember, this is what took Stephen to the next level.

CHALLENGE 2

Do a little something extra for your work as if you were working for Jesus. This can be for your household if you are a homemaker.

CHALLENGE 3

Do something special for a relationship that is important to you. It doesn't need to be a lot just a little extra.

BIBLE READING FOR TODAY

Spend some time thinking a little deeper about Colossians 3:23–24.

Jot down any impressions you feel God puts on your heart.

_____
_____
_____
_____
_____
_____
_____

Day 22

EMBRACE RADICAL OBEDIENCE

As a good podcast producer, you like to mix it up from time to time. For today's podcast, you decide to host a panel discussion. One at a time, the time machine brings your three guests. The first guest for the panel is a return guest: Noah. The second guest is the prophet Isaiah, and the third guest is Matthew, the disciple of Jesus. You sit around your dining room table and set up a microphone in front of your guests.

Since Noah was the first to arrive, he starts. His is a familiar story of building an ark and animals and the first rainbow. But since you covered that in the last podcast, you dig a little deeper. It pays off when he shares about the process of building the ark. He goes into more detail talking about the one hundred years it took to make that big boat.

You have a hard time imagining working on something for that long for an event in history you didn't completely understand. Day after day, month after month, Noah would work. Months turned into years, and years turned into decades. Noah said he was just being obedient to what God had said to him.

Embrace Radical Obedience

Next to speak is the prophet Isaiah. He amazes everyone with the story of when he saw God on his throne while he was in the temple. He pulls you into the drama as he shares about his interactions with King Hezekiah. He then turns to a story you don't remember hearing about.

God used Isaiah to write some of the great word pictures of the Bible. But this time God made Isaiah himself the word picture of the judgment to come on his people. God told him to walk around naked. For three years, he was a reminder to people everywhere he went. Visiting the king and his nephew's birthday party got a little more awkward. It was hard, but he had heard from God and was being obedient.

Matthew astutely picks up on the theme that seems to be developing. He shares the story of obedience he has told many times before. Matthew knew that he wasn't liked by many because he was a tax collector. Even his mother would give him grief every day he went to work. People who didn't know him were friendly right up to the moment when he got to his tax-collecting booth.

> **A MOMENT OF OBEDIENCE CAN CHANGE YOUR LIFE.**

Even though Matthew wanted to serve God, his job meant that none of the religious folk would be his friend. Some nationalist zealots had even threatened his life. So when he wasn't working, he hung out with other people on the edge: town drunks, crooks, and the ladies of the night.

One day when Matthew was sitting in his booth, Jesus walked by where he was working. He said two words to Matthew: "Follow me." In that moment, he got up and left it all to follow Jesus. It was a moment of obedience that changed his life.

Each podcast guest illustrates a type of obedience God might be calling you to right now.

Noah teaches us the importance of *long* obedience. Sometimes, God's call requires our day-in and day-out obedience over a long period of time. We may not even see the results we like. The prophet Jeremiah is another example of this type of obedience. From a young age, he spoke the messages that God told him to say, and nobody ever seemed to listen. Would you give up after a while?

Isaiah gives us an example of *hard* obedience. God asked him to do something difficult. Often, God asked people in the Bible to do something hard. Abraham being asked to sacrifice Isaac was another example of this type of obedience. Sometimes, God asks us to do something that is not easy.

Matthew shows us what *quick* obedience looks like. This is obedience where you must act right away. The moment will pass if you don't act now. Don't wait around thinking about it or the opportunity may pass.

THOUGHT FOR THE DAY

Obedience is often the prerequisite price tag to experience true adventure with Jesus.

CHALLENGE 1

Have you stopped being obedient to something God has called you to do because it is taking a long time to finish? Ask God if you should still be doing it. If you sense "yes," do something today to get the process going again.

CHALLENGE 2

Is there something that God has told you to do that you haven't done yet because it is going to be hard? Will you dare do something about it today?

CHALLENGE 3

Is there something that you know you should do but have been procrastinating for some reason or the other? Are you struggling with immediate obedience? Or are you daring enough to ask God if He has something for you to do today? Then do it!

BIBLE READING FOR TODAY

Psalm 32:8

Jot down any impressions you feel God puts on your heart.

_____
_____
_____
_____
_____
_____
_____
_____

Day 23

DEAL WITH A SIN

One of the more unique conversations you could have on your time-travel podcast would be to bring back both Samson and Delilah for a couple's conversation. Or maybe, so you don't get too many fireworks, you could just interview them one at a time.

We're feeling bold today. Let's interview both, together. Samson arrives first, dressed in prison clothes, blind, head shaven, a shell of his former strongman's body. As he looks back at his life, frustration is a common theme. "I really had the potential to be one of the great ones," he says. When he could keep his act together, that is. He goes totally silent, lost in thought. Feeling a bit awkward, you begin to interview Delilah, seated as far from Samson as she can get.

Delilah is as arrogant and as beautiful as you imagined. She is movie-star beautiful, she and Samson must have made quite the couple. For a while. Throughout the interview, Delilah returns to how easy it was to trick Samson with the same things women have used to tempt men throughout history. She played to his weaknesses, and she wore him down over time. She laughs at how stupid Samson must seem to all of us.

Samson, on the other hand, is not laughing at all. Regret is all over his face. He knew his area of weakness, but he figured he could play with fire one more time. As the interview wraps up,

Deal with a Sin

he begs you to go back to a time before he met Delilah so he could make a different choice. Sadly, that is not an option (space-time continuum, for all of my nerd friends).

When I read accounts of people like Samson in the Bible, I sometimes wish the story could end differently. Yet, every time I read it, it ends the same way. They can't change the ending of their story because their story is already done being written.

> **YOUR STORY IS NOT OVER. YOU CAN STILL CHANGE THE ENDING.**

This should be a huge challenge to us. If you are reading this right now, your story is not over. No matter where you are, you can still change the ending. The sin you may be in today does not need to define who you become. The question is, will you take the opportunity that many in history would love to have?

THOUGHT FOR THE DAY

The sin you are in right now
does not need to define the rest of your life.

For some of you this may be the toughest challenge yet. But it also could do the most long-term good. Today's challenge may take a while to sort out, but the important thing is to do something today.

CHALLENGE 1

There may be a sin in your life that quickly comes to mind that you know you have not dealt with yet. You may need to have a conversation with a trusted friend. You may need to get rid of something in your life.

CHALLENGE 2

Sin is not always about what we are doing. Sometimes, sin is about what we *aren't* doing. Going back to our previous podcast, are you still wrestling with God about an area of disobedience in your life?

CHALLENGE 3

Nothing may come to mind when it comes to the area of sin. That doesn't mean there is nothing there. I dare you to ask God to search your heart and reveal to you any areas that He wants to deal with.

BIBLE READING FOR TODAY

Judges 16

Jot down any impressions you feel God puts on your heart.

_____
_____
_____
_____
_____
_____
_____

Day 24

TAKE A RISK

The day you invite Queen Esther to your time-travel podcast is a bit of a mess. First, her royal administration sends a guard detail to secure your house. Then, when she actually arrives, her entourage of servants fills the house to standing-room only. You are surprised at how weird it feels to have royalty in your house. The production is almost a bit much.

As the interview begins, you feel relieved to have survived the pageantry thus far. Esther shares how she became queen: a beauty contest. The same overwhelming feeling you experienced before today's podcast, Esther experienced ten times over the first time she entered the palace.

This story in mind, I asked my daughter Samantha what she would ask Queen Esther, and she wanted to know what it felt like when Esther was finally chosen as queen. It would have been a day she would never forget.

There are many lessons to learn from Esther, but I want you to think about the right time to take a risk. I once heard Professor Vijay Govindarajan of Dartmouth (cool name!) encourage people to take low-cost risks. This is good advice, but Queen Esther was given the choice of a high-stakes risk that could cost her everything. She could enter the king's presence without him asking which could cost her life, or sit back and do nothing and risk the lives of all of the Jewish people. She was wise about it and set the stage, but the risk level was still very high.

The other question my daughter wanted to ask Queen Esther was what it felt like to tell the king her true identity. I can only imagine that her heart was pounding. Sometimes, you have to take a risk.

One of my missions as leader of Christ Connection is to engage 100,000 people to pray for pastors and leaders. This is a risky, all-consuming mission that will take effort over a period of time, but I am doing something almost every day to help this vision become a reality. There are risks we take that create before and after moments with God.

Other causes are only a part of our lives. You may support a ministry through volunteering, prayer, financial giving, or words of encouragement. I support a ministry called Live Dead because I am passionate about planting churches in some of the most difficult places in the world. This said, my involvement with Live Dead doesn't consume me like my mission to raise up 100,000 people to pray for pastors and leaders.

> **THERE ARE RISKS WE TAKE THAT CREATE BEFORE AND AFTER MOMENTS WITH GOD.**

What are the causes God has given you?

Does your church already support a cause you could pitch in to help as part of being Jesus' hands and feet?

Do you have a child or family member with a need that pushes you into helping others with the same need?

Maybe God has been putting something on your heart for a while, but you have never started.

THOUGHT FOR THE DAY

*The causes that burn in our heart
should drive us to our knees.*

Today, I challenge you to do something about a cause you have in your heart. Take a risk and let it impact you.

CHALLENGE 1

Send a message to someone in an organization (like a church or other ministry) to see how you can help out. Do a little research to really understand the need and let the cause grab your heart.

CHALLENGE 2

If God has put on your heart to actually start a new ministry, do something. This may include a call or message to your pastor to start a conversation, or a call or message to a similar ministry to see what you can learn from them. This process may take a while, but do something to get the ball rolling.

CHALLENGE 3

Already involved in a cause? Do something to move the cause a little bit forward. Let a friend who might be interested in this know about it. Share something about it in your social media world. Take a risk.

BIBLE READING FOR TODAY

Esther 4:12–17

Jot down any impressions you feel God puts on your heart.

Day 25

FACE YOUR FEARS

I love how the Bible is filled with all sort of different types of people. We often encounter people who at first glance would seem like weird heroes. As you crank up the trusty time machine today, you are introduced to Rahab. She is known mainly for her encounter in the book of Joshua with the spies sent to Jericho.

Rahab's story is almost a subplot in the high stakes adventure that is the opening of the book of Joshua. I mentioned that my last name was made up by a relative, but I didn't mention that part of it is found in the Sinhala Bible. *Senapathi* is the same word for "commander of the army" who we see instructing Joshua on the plan to take Jericho. The plan he receives does not seem connected to the information collected from the spies in Joshua chapter two. But here Rahab sits in front of you.

Now I have called her Rahab up to this point. Most times, when she is talked about, the word *prostitute* is connected to her name. Prostitute is not a word that works well in most children's church lessons. I even hesitated putting her story in this book for fear of losing my PG status. But if you were sitting across the kitchen table from her, my guess is that her story would have engaged you.

Your research for the interview would not pull up much about her past other than the title attached to her name. How she got to that point, we are not told. You would have found that her family lived in town and that she was unmarried. The town was all abuzz with talk about the Israelites, but other than that, it probably started as an ordinary day.

Since there was no *Super 8 Motel* in Jericho, her place doubled as an inn. Now apparently these two spies were no James Bond, since it says the king of Jericho knew where they were and where they were staying. Rahab knew who they were as well when she welcomed them into her home. Believing the God of Israel over the god of the people where she lived, she hid the spies. It was a moment of courage.

There is no indication that at the beginning of that week, she was planning on helping the spies. As you ask her questions, you realize that this was just a step of faith. Sometimes, acts of faith are played out over years like the story of Abraham and Sarah.

ACTS OF FAITH REQUIRE US TO FACE DOWN FEAR AND DO IT ANYWAY.

Other times, like the story told you by Rahab, we exercise our faith in brief, life-changing moments. It is like the idea in the movie *We Bought a Zoo* where the Matt Damon character says, "You know, sometimes all you need is twenty seconds of insane courage. Just literally twenty seconds of just embarrassing bravery. And I promise you, something great will come of it."

Rahab tells you her act of courage changed her life. She gets a little teary-eyed thinking about how that moment saved her and her family. What she couldn't have known was that both the authors of the New Testament books of Hebrews and James use her as an example of courage and faith. Hebrews even lists her in the "Hall of Fame" of people of faith.

The Bible and church history are filled with people who faced

Face Your Fears

their fear and took steps of faith. Acts of faith require us to face down fear and do it anyway. We don't know when our Rahab moment will come. We want our courage muscle to be in shape when it arrives. Even if we start small, Rahab would tell you that when the moment comes, you will be glad you were ready.

THOUGHT FOR THE DAY

The time for building your courage is before you need it.

Your goal today is to face a fear, large or small. The goal is to feel your heart pounding a little bit.

CHALLENGE 1

If you are an introvert, try starting a conversation with someone in a store or some other place you wouldn't normally reach out. If you are an extrovert, try another time of solitude and silence.

CHALLENGE 2

Try something new. It doesn't need to feel like a "spiritual" challenge. Go climb a tree or try a new food or restaurant that has always made you nervous. Today is the day.

CHALLENGE 3

God may have a spiritual challenge for you. For example, go up to someone you know and say, "Is there anything I can pray for you today?" And then pray for them.

BIBLE READING FOR TODAY

Joshua 2

Jot down any impressions you feel God puts on your heart.

Day 26

MAKE A GOODNESS AND MERCY TIMELINE

The unique thing about being an interviewer is you never know what areas of a person's life are going to become the theme of your conversation. Anyone you talk to has a long history from which to draw. Today's guest, the Apostle Paul, is no exception. You spent the night before reading all of his letters and have a long list of questions ready for whichever direction the conversation goes.

To warm up, you ask about Paul's background, his religious upbringing, and his training under the great rabbi, Gamaliel. As you scan down your questions expecting to talk about Paul's early ministry days, he goes down a road you didn't expect to spend a lot of time on: his time of persecuting the church.

He talks about the pivotal moment when he is involved in the stoning of Stephen. He remembers it so well. Tears fill his eyes as he takes you through that time in his life. Paul shares of the hate and terror that he began to inflict on Christians. He rounded up a band of thugs and poured on the passion with which they would do their work. He organized "sanctified terror" with some semblance of order, meeting with the religious leaders of the day to get reference letters to do his work in other towns. He describes with sadness the pounding on doors and the arrests that were made.

Yet, after describing this terrible story, Paul says, "By God's grace, those past moments helped make me who I am today."

The Holy Spirit brings to mind a verse you read the night before: "For I am the least of the apostles and do not even deserve to be called an apostle, because I persecuted the church of God. But by the grace of God I am what I am, and his grace to me was not without effect. No, I worked harder than all of them—yet not I, but the grace of God that was with me" (1 Corinthians 15:9–10). Paul realizes that his past made him work harder in the present and allows God's grace to flow.

This is a powerful truth. Paul is not proud of his past. He is not happy about it, but he does allow God's grace to be applied to it. You may be thinking of something in your past you would love to go back and change. Hearing the pain you may have caused I might want to send you back, too. But Paul says that since we can't do that the next best thing is to let God apply His grace to it.

It reminds me of the *Star Trek* episode where a time-traveling trickster, named "Q," gives Captain Jean-Luc Picard the chance to change a "bad" decision he made in the past. As to not lose you who are not Star Trek fans, I will just say changing the past kept Picard from ultimately becoming captain. One of my college professors, in speaking about this episode and the verses from Paul that we just read, reminded us that even if we could change the past, we might not want to anyway.

> **WHEN WE ARE NOT HAPPY WITH OUR PAST WE MUST ALLOW GRACE TO BE APPLIED TO IT.**

It reminds me of my years as a pastor. I was a senior pastor for nine years. During that time I pastored three different churches. I closed two of the churches, and at the third church, I only lasted for a year and a half. Sometimes, I think about things I would have changed if I could do it over again. But if I changed those things, I might not be writing this today. My experience as a small-church pastor has given me empathy and a means to connect with small-church pastors, and a fire in my heart to raise up 100,000 people to pray for pastors! Would I love to go back and change some things? Of course I would! But since I can't, I might as well let God apply his grace to that.

Today, as you have been reading this, a mistake you made long ago or last week may come to mind. Whether a onetime event or a recurring habit, whether a sin or just a bad decision you wish you could take back, today is the day to apply God's grace to it.

Our past is a great conversation starter with God. My pastor in high school liked to remind us that the Bible says, ". . . surely goodness and mercy will follow me all the days of my life" (Psalm 23:6 ESV). He would then say that when we look back, we should see goodness and mercy.

THOUGHT FOR THE DAY

We can't change the past but we can see God's grace in it.

Just one challenge for today. Make it your own.

CHALLENGE

Marilu Henner, in her fun book *Total Memory Makeover*, challenges people to make a timeline of their own lives. This is a fun project, but for today, you are starting with a simple "goodness and mercy timeline."

Find something on which to capture your thoughts. It could be a notebook or an electronic device.

Pray that God would remind you of times when He showed mercy and goodness to you in your life.

Jot down times of mercy and goodness that come to mind as you go through your day. Even for some of the darkest times of your life, look for ways that, if not for God's goodness and mercy, those moments could have been a whole lot worse. See how many you can come up with in one day.

BIBLE READING FOR TODAY

Psalm 23

Jot down any impressions you feel God puts on your heart.

_____

_____

_____

_____

_____

_____

_____

_____

_____

Day 27

ENJOY YOUR CHURCH

As someone who has "embraced the nerd within," I can tell you a supervillain is an antagonist who takes ordinary villainy to the next level. A supervillain goes beyond tying up the hero and planning a clever escape. Supervillains aren't satisfied until they have destroyed the world.

Taking a break from interviewing heroes, today you interview Achan, infamous for hoarding forbidden items for himself. The Israelites lost God's protection, and their next battle turned into a disastrous loss (Joshua 7).

The strange thing is that when you sit down with Achan, he seems like an ordinary guy. He doesn't seem like a villain, much less a supervillain. He doesn't even seem to have mastered the classic villain laugh. Selfish and self-absorbed maybe, but take-over-the-world crazy? Not really. Achan just seemed more concerned about his own interests than the impact he had on his community.

> **SOMETIMES WE MISS THE CONNECTION OUR ACTIONS HAVE ON THOSE AROUND US.**

Sitting down with Achan is an important reminder at this point in the book. Like Achan, we sometimes miss the connection our actions have on those around us. Many of your daily

103

challenges in this book have focused on your connection to a local body of believers: a church. Let's focus here a bit.

Paul refers to the local church as a "body." Your church family is like a body with many parts, and one person's action has an impact on the others. The church *is* a "family," just one formed by the blood of Jesus, not a traditional familial tie. If you're not a part of a church family, I challenge you to move in that direction today. They need you as much as you need them. God wants to use your unique story, talents, and gifts to bless the other "parts of the body." Don't think they won't bless you, too!

A cautionary tale but not a guilt trip, Achan's story reminds us of the opportunity to take action and make a difference. I love the quote from Bill Hybels, "The local church is the hope of the world." When it is functioning properly, the local church can be the best expression of Jesus that people will see. Achan's story reminds us we each play a part in that expression.

THOUGHT FOR THE DAY

God has given His church to be a blessing in your life. Are you a blessing to them?

CHALLENGE 1

If you are not a part of a local church, make an effort to find one. A suggestion: rather than "shopping" for a church to meet your needs, look for a church where you can find a place to serve.

CHALLENGE 2

If you are a part of a local congregation, what is one small thing you could do to be a blessing to someone in the "family" today? Do it today!

CHALLENGE 3

People often serve in a church for a long time without many thanks. Think of someone serving in your church. Write them a thank-you note.

BIBLE READING FOR TODAY

Joshua 7

Jot down any impressions you feel God puts on your heart.

_____
_____
_____
_____
_____
_____
_____
_____
_____
_____
_____

Day 28

KEEP THE DREAM ALIVE

Part of your job as an interviewer is to understand the emotional state of your guests. The emotions are part of what makes the audio recordings come alive. You are getting pretty good at knowing when to push a little deeper and when to give your guests a few moments to collect themselves.

When Hannah comes through the time machine, you can tell drawing out her emotions is not going to be a challenge. Hannah shows a full range of emotions and is not afraid to express her feelings. As you sit down to record, she points out that emotions are an important part of her story.

At first as you listen to her story, you have a hard time relating to her position in life as one of two wives of a man in Israel (1 Samuel 1). But as you keep going, you realize she is like any other person. Her culture looked down on women who could not have kids, and she was struggling with infertility. To make matters worse, her husband's other wife tormented Hannah at every occasion. It broke Hannah's heart because having kids was her dream. Not being able to have kids wore on her emotions.

I understand a little of what this situation is like. For the first ten years of our marriage, Jen and I didn't have any children. A doctor told us we would never be able to have children. So when

Samantha came along, we were thankful for the miracle of her life.

But ten years is long enough to understand a little of the emotion that Hannah might have felt. I remember the pain Jen would carry back from baby showers. There were good days and bad days. The emotion of carrying a dream can feel heavy at times.

You may not struggle with infertility, but I imagine you are waiting on God for *something*. God has given all of us dreams, and we carry some for a long time. I love the first line of the poem "The Ode" by Arthur O'Shaughnessy: "We are the music-makers, And we are the dreamers of dreams . . ."[3] God has put dreams in all of us.

"But what do I do when I carry the dream, yet nothing seems to be happening?" you ask Hannah. She tells you she went into the presence of God and poured out her emotion to God. She didn't try to hide her pain from God but brought the dream to God in prayer. Hannah dabs a tear from her eye. You pause the recording and grab her a tissue.

> **THE SAFEST PLACE TO BRING OUR DREAMS IS TO GOD WHO GAVE THEM TO US.**

The safest place to bring our dreams is to God, who gave them to us. Hannah didn't deny her emotions and frustration, but at the same time she didn't let the emotion cause her to forget her dream. Hannah may not be able to tell you why some dreams are fulfilled and some take a long time, but as she tells you about her son Samuel impacting the nation, she is grateful she kept taking her dream to God.

THOUGHT FOR THE DAY

We bring our dreams to the God who gave them to us.

CHALLENGE 1

Write out a dream that God has given to you. Find a place to put it that you can revisit it when you get discouraged. Sometimes, we can forget our dreams when we don't take time to write them down.

CHALLENGE 2

Maybe, the idea of a dream seems a little lofty, and you can't think of anything. Rather than worry if something is really a dream or not, write out some of the desires of your heart. Start praying in the days to come about which are your desires and which are things that God has placed in your heart.

CHALLENGE 3

Hannah experienced the fulfillment of her desire that she poured out to God. Maybe, you have experienced God answering a prayer like that in your life. Take some time today and really go over it in your mind and thank God for His answer to prayer.

BIBLE READING FOR TODAY

1 Samuel 1

Jot down any impressions you feel God puts on your heart.

Day 29

LIVE WITH THE BIBLE OVER A LIFETIME

I once traveled to spend a day with one of my mentors, Dick Eastman. Dick has served as the president of Every Home for Christ and also a member of the National Prayer Committee. We spent some time talking, and he also showed me part of his headquarters. But one of the highlights for me was when we prayed together.

Dick prayed something over me that has stuck with me ever since. Quoting from John Wesley, he prayed that I would be known as a man of "one book." He was praying that I would be known for my love of the Bible.

Now, I am grateful that you bought this book, and I may write others (so I am not suggesting that you never buy another book). But I pray that you too would be known for your love of the Bible.

Today you are going to interview Joshua, for whom a book of the Bible is named. Joshua is a military and civic leader, a man of action and adventure. He led the Israelites in to take the Promised Land. He would have known how to make commands and lead people.

But God had an important instruction for Joshua: "Do not let this Book of the Law depart from your mouth; meditate on it day and night, so that you may be careful to do everything written in it. Then you will be prosperous and successful" (Joshua 1:8). Joshua tells you that his time in the Book was as important as anything he ever did.

In our "busy" society, we need to be creative to make sure we find ways to keep getting God's Word into our lives. Let me encourage you to think creatively about how you can let God's Word speak to you. Here are just a few ways.

> **CONSISTENCY IS MORE IMPORTANT THAN AN IMPRESSIVE BEGINNING AND THEN FLAMING OUT.**

Memorize the Bible. I could nerd out on the powerful systems you can use to memorize Scripture, but for now pick a Psalm and work on memorizing it.

Listen to the Bible. If you commute to work in the morning, you could listen to a large portion of scripture every week. Considering the length of most people's commutes, they could listen through the Bible every year and still have time for their favorite podcast.

Character studies. Take some time and spend it with one of the people of the Bible. Spend a whole month with Esther or Gideon.

Slow reading. Believers throughout history have practiced taking a small passage of the Bible and letting it work through them over a period of time.

I could go on talking about praying the Scripture or word studies, but I don't want to overwhelm you. Consistency is more important than an impressive beginning and then flaming out.

THOUGHT FOR THE DAY

One word from God could change your life forever.
Aren't you glad He has given us a whole book?

Try something new with Scripture.

CHALLENGE 1

Pick a passage you are going to work on memorizing. This can be a series of verses or a whole passage. You can even find a tool to help you with your memorization. At the time of this writing, my favorite app is called Remember Me.

CHALLENGE 2

Pick a book of the Bible to listen to, something you could download and finish before you got home tonight. Most would easily be listened to in a week.

CHALLENGE 3

Pick a person from the Bible that you have met in this book that you would like to learn more about. Journey with them for a week or month. You can study more about them but also just think about how they would react in situations that you encounter.

BIBLE READING FOR TODAY

Psalm 119 (I know this is the longest chapter in the Bible. You can do it!).

Jot down any impressions you feel God puts on your heart.

Day 30

ASK GOD FOR A CHALLENGE

After what I prayerfully expect has been a life-changing month for you, we have arrived at our last day of this journey together! I hope this journey has been encouraging and challenging all at the same time. But I don't want you to miss out on this last challenge and this last podcast interview. Before we close up the time machine, I want to bring to you Peter, the disciple of Jesus.

Peter has a lot of opinions. Of all of the disciples, he seemed to have a lot to say. Now, he tells you stories that make you laugh as you think about how silly he must have sounded to Jesus. You shed a few tears as Peter retells the story of his denial of Jesus as his master's life was in the balance. You turn off the microphone to catch your breath when he describes how Jesus turned and looked at him in that moment.

Peter gets a lot of grief for his response during a different episode of his life, but I am not sure that he should be given such a hard time. When the disciples are all in the boat together and Jesus comes to them walking on the water, it must have been amazing. Peter then says to Jesus, "Lord if it's you, tell me to come to you on the water" (Matthew 14:28).

Peter tells you this story from the beginning and humbly admits he began to sink after a while. He downplays that he

Ask God for a Challenge

obediently followed Jesus into a place where physical laws are optional. Peter walked on water and no one else even got out of the boat. I have never walked on water. Have you? Peter walked away that day with a faith lesson and an epic story to tell his grandkids.

This leads us to a final lesson and challenge.

Peter asked Jesus to tell him to come on the water. He saw Jesus do it, and he wanted to do it as well. I think that, in that moment, Peter knew that if he didn't ask, he would regret it for the rest of his life. I wonder if some of the others in the boat kicked themselves for not asking Jesus as well. Let's be the kind of people who ask to get out of the boat.

> **LET'S BE THE KIND OF PEOPLE WHO ASK TO GET OUT OF THE BOAT.**

THOUGHT FOR THE DAY

God wants to use us and to stretch us.

Each day of this book, I have ended with giving you a few challenges. I hope that some of them have pushed you outside of your comfort zone. I hope that God added some extra challenges to you as well along the way. In this case, we need to be like Peter and ask God for challenges for our everyday life.

CHALLENGE

I hope you will do today's challenge every day for the rest of your life. Ask God what His challenge is for you and, as you read your Bible, ask God what He has for you to do that day. Then, as you go through your day, try to be aware of the nudges He gives you for that moment. My closing thought? Let me give you the advice that Jesus' mother told some people who were about to go on an adventure with Jesus: "Do whatever he tells you." (John 2:5)

BIBLE READING FOR TODAY

Matthew 14:22-33

Jot down any impressions you feel God puts on your heart.

CURTAIN CALL

Mom and Dad – From childhood you taught me to live a life of radical obedience to God. Thank you.

The Christ Connection Board – During the time of putting together this book, your wisdom and direction helped me see the big picture on life and ministry.

My Emmanuel connect group – I am glad we get to do life together.

Chris MacKinnon – All of my books are better because of you. Christ Connection would not be where it is today without you.

Emmanuel Staff – Thanks for letting me hang out with you and be "pseudo staff" on such a great team.

Amanda Pikala – Thank you for letting me process this book with you so that it is more authentic.

Andrew Black – Thanks for continuing to work on this in a crazy season of life. I appreciate you journeying inside my head.

Kelly Black – Thanks for helping me dream with this book. It is a part of changing the world.

David Nithang – Your friendship is an inspiration.

Dr. Marvin Smith – For your help with the chapter on Paul and Q. Some lessons stay with you forever.

Tim Ferriss – Your books have helped me give expression to my faith.

The Dude Perfect Crew – Thank you for setting an example of creative faith. Pound it. Head noggin.

Kevin Olson and Auto Glass Professionals – Thanks for helping with the book launch.

The Committees (Assemblies of God, National Prayer, Minnesota) – Being a part of your tribe pushes me to make a bigger impact.

My prayer team – This book literally would not exist without you.

My book review team – Thanks for making this better.

The Christ Connection Financial Supporters – You are the oxygen of this ministry.

To the friends, family, and mentors who help me along in life– It would take another book to list all of you!

My daughter, Samantha – Thank you for the inspiration and our many talks about books.

My wife, Jen – I love you! I am so glad we get to journey through life together.

To my God – I am grateful you gave me the opportunity to write this book.

A SPECIAL NOTE TO PASTORS AND LEADERS

When I started the ministry of Christ Connection back in 2005 I had just finished 9 years as a senior pastor. I have sat where you sit. Although I wrote this book with the goal to help the individual Christian experience a new level in their walk with God: you were in the back of my mind. Each day the reader of this book is challenged to take some specific action based on the word of God. How exciting would it be to see your whole church or ministry with a flurry of activity for 30 days? That idea is one of the things that most excites me about this book.

If you choose to do this as a church here are a few notes:

Help people with the challenges. Maybe use your Sunday service as a time for people to do the activity of that day. For example, if Sunday lands on Day 6 (Encourage Someone) try to include that in your service. How fun could it be to just take 5 minutes in the service and have people encourage as many people as they can?

Be aware that the design of this book is to take people on an adventure with Jesus. This may open up some long dormant dreams that God has placed in their heart. They may come to you for council and advice. Let me encourage you to help them focus on next steps. This will keep them moving and from premature starts of ministries from people who are not ready.

This book is about starting something. Consider that as you place this book in your church calendar. For many the beginning of the year would be a great place. But you know your group. Maybe the beginning of the summer would be a good fit or the beginning of the school year. It might even be a great starting point as you have the new beginnings of Easter.

After you have completed the journey, I would love to hear from you. If you would send me a note and let me know how it helped you it would mean a lot. You can find our contact info at *www.christconnection.cc.*

Thanks for going on an adventure with your church! May God bless your efforts.

End Notes

1. Lecrae. "Unashamed." Audio blog post. The Art of Charm, 25 August 2016.

2. Foster, Richard J. "Solitude and Wide, Open Spaces" *Renovaré*. 14 March 2016. Web. 18 December 2016.

3. O'Shaughnessy, Arthur. "Ode." *Poetry Foundation*, https://www.poetryfoundation.org/poems/54933/ode-. Accessed on 18 December 2016.

Other Books by Kevin Senapatiratne

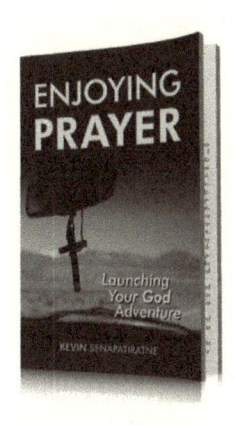

ENJOYING PRAYER

Do you find prayer boring? It was never designed to be that way.

Join Kevin as he takes you through a journey of simple ideas to help make prayer a "get to" before it is a "have to."

Charles Finney's
LECTURES ON REVIVAL:

Kevin has been deeply impacted by the life and ministry of Charles Finney. Finney's ministry had a great impact on the church in the United States.

Not able to find Finney's most important book in print, Kevin condensed and updated it for today's reader. If you would like to experience a revival this book gives you the steps.

Christ Connection

After 9 years as a senior pastor, in 2005, Kevin started the ministry of *Christ Connection* to help ignite pastors and churches through the power of prayer ministry here and around the world.

Filled with the desire to see every Christian experience the full life that is possible with God we:

- Create resources online to encourage and equip Christians for a powerful and practical adventure with Jesus.
- Provide conferences, seminars and services to help the local church go to the next level with God
- Assist pastors and ministry leaders to help them develop a culture of prayer in their church or organization.

To learn more about Kevin and *Christ Connection*, visit us online at *www.christconnection.cc*.